# what people are saying

No matter where you are on your journey in ministry, Valley's are inevitable. When you find yourself there, Tom's book is your guide not just out of it, but how to grow and flourish within it, so your next mountain top experience will be all the richer for the time you spent in the valley. I can't recommend this highly enough no matter where you are on your hike through life. It's a book that will help bring healing and hope to those who find themselves in a challenging season of ministry. Tom's heart for hurting pastors comes through on every page. He has been where you are, and is eager to graciously walk with you to higher ground.

> *Pastor Karl Bastian*
> *Founder of Kidology.org*
> *Host of YosemiteSummit.org*

I have known Tom Bump for several years, I am honored to have coached him and walk with him through his journey. I am also honored to call him a friend. Tom is the real deal and I am thankful Jesus has instructed him to write this book "Valleys Over Mountains." Within these pages are pure gold. Words of wisdom and hope from someone who has lived this and has come out not only stronger but better with a burning mandate to "help restore others!" I wish a resource like this existed years ago. This book will help transform you from burnout to blastoff and give you the tools to stay the course toward healthy ministry. I highly recommend this book and Tom's ministry "Restoring Leaders"

> *Jim Wideman*
> *Kidmin Pioneer, author, speaker, coach & pastor*
> *Jim Wideman Ministries*
> *Nashville, TN*

Every leader needs someone in their corner to help them navigate through the season that we aren't sharing in social media statuses. In Valleys Over Mountains, Tom Bump is that for you just like he is with leaders every day."

> *Terry Weaver,*
> *Founder of The Thing & Author of Making Elephants Fly*

We've all faced challenging seasons. Days turn into weeks, weeks turn into months and it feels as if you'll never make it out of the valley. We all yearn to experience the overwhelming sense of victory that comes with mountaintop moments. We want the warmth of the sun shining on our face and the sound of exuberant congratulations filling our ears. Yet, for many of us, the mountaintops are few and far between and oftentimes we find ourselves in the valley. In Tom Bump's book, Valleys Over Mountains, you will learn how to embrace the valley. The scripture references, reflective questions and challenging insights will help you see your current season as not only surmountable, but also necessary. Through personal experience, Tom paints a difficult, but purposeful way to walk in the valley. Readers of this book will find peace and comfort and learn how to make the most of every season in which they face.

*Jessica Bealer   Director of Family Ministry Services*
*Generis*
*www.generis.com*

As someone who is addicted to hustle, and has to schedule time on his calendar to stop, pray, and listen to the spirit, I appreciated the practical application and incredible wisdom in Valleys Over Mountains. Life, and especially leadership, has its ups and downs. But God calls us to lead, and love, and thrive, no matter the season or challenge before us. Tom's book is an encouragement and practical guide to help you thrive through the highs and lows.

*Justin Dean,*
*Creator of That Church Conference and SundayU.com*

It's a joy to be on the mountain top.  But what about the valleys?  We tend to shy away from talking about those experiences.  But Tom shows us the many lessons we can learn in the valleys and how it will propel you to a closer walk with your Savior.  Reading this book will totally change how you view trials and hard times. It's in the valley we grow closer to God and learn to depend on Him more and more.

*Dale Hudson, Founder and President of BCM*
*www.buildingchildrensministry.com*

I have spent 25 years at one location ministering to kids. I have spent time on the mountain top. I have spent even more time in the valley. Tom is right, valleys are better.

We ALL face valleys in life and ministry, the question is how we respond to God and others while we are there. Tom has done a masterful job walking us through a biblical and practical approach to fulfillment when things don't go like we planned. Each chapter is a gold mine of real life insight where he speaks directly from his heart and God's word. You will find this book encouraging, challenging and incredibly insightful as you journey through your own valley. Especially helpful are the questions at the end of each chapter. They are brilliantly written and get you thinking about the exact things you need to be thinking through and processing as you grow in Christ in the shadow of the mountain top.

Don't waste any moment of the valley experience. Take the insights from this book and apply them. When you do, I know you will agree with Tom, and me... valleys ARE better.

> Mike Johnson
> Kids Pastor, Executive Producer ISeeIt! Productions

"Tom has a way of sharing his valleys with authenticity, hope, and Biblical guidance. Whether you're in a valley now, coming out of one, or preparing for your next one, this book will be encouraging, challenging, inspiring, and hope-filled. Grab it, read it, then buy one for a friend. We all need this message. And Tom is a wonderful guide."

> Keith Ferrin
> Author/Speaker/Messaging Coach
> www.keithferrin.com

To be honest we've all walked through some of the valleys of life when we wished for mountaintop experiences instead. Sometimes our journeys through the valleys are so deep and so long that it seems like we can't even see the mountain tops. Our eyes are focused on struggles of trying to make it through the valleys.

In this book, my friend and ministry colleague, Tom Bump, takes us through his own valley experiences with honesty, and yet with clarity and with a sense of compassion and empathy. I know Tom well enough to know that he's been there. Life has presented him with very real and very difficult journeys through the valleys.

But, here Tom's story helps the reader see God's hand and God's loving direction even through our own time in the valleys. I love Tom's approach in this book – he writes with integrity and shares his own life experiences with sometimes brutal humility and truthfulness.

Tom writes as one who has lived his message. He's gone through the valleys and can look back on those valley experiences with a sense of victory and purpose. The key thing about Tom's book, and his life, is that he has walked this journey, he has stayed close to God through the tough times, and he shares real-life and Biblically-based principles to help us walk through our own valleys.

I highly recommend this book, and Tom's ministry to you.

*Mel Walker,*
*Co-founder and President*
*Vision For Youth and*
*author of "Going On For God"*

# valleys over mountains

## A GUIDE THROUGH THE HARD SEASONS

TOM BUMP

**A RESTORING LEADERS PUBLICATION**
www.restoringleaders.org

**Valleys Over Mountains: A Guide Through the Hard Seasons**

Published by Restoring Leaders
4515 Mel Ln.
Wooster, Ohio 44691

Printed in the United States of America

Visit our website **www.restoringleaders.org**

**Credits:**
Editors: John & Melissa Tillman
Cover: Simon Parry
Interior Design: Nicole Jones

ISBN 979-8-9851057-0-4 (Paperback)

ISBN 979-8-9851057-1-1 (ePub)

# about the author

Tom and his wife April, have four young adult children. Tom has been in ministry for over thirty years. He has served in churches across four states, ranging in attendance from 50 up to 5,000. Tom has served in many positions, from Interim Lead Pastor, to Children's Pastor, and many other roles.

Tom is also the founder and lead coach for Restoring Leaders that offers retreats and online care groups to help hurting or burned out ministry leaders get back in and stay in ministry.

He is the host of The Kids Ministry Collective Podcast and administers its Facebook group.

Tom is also the Lead Coach for KMC Coaching where he helps leaders learn and lead the way God designed.

Tom also speaks nationally at ministry conferences, camps, training programs, and anywhere the good Lord opens the door to share.

# dedications

To my wife April, my earthly best friend. There are no words that can express what you mean to me. I would not be where I am without you by my side. You've pushed and pulled me through many dark times when many would have walked away. You worked so many hours of overtime just to give me the freedom to serve those in ministry. I am confident you will hear "well done good and faithful servant!" from our Savior. I love you!

To my kids, Tom, Alyssa, Andrew, and Tara. I'm sorry you had to watch your father walk through so many dark valleys. I can only pray and trust my God to protect your hearts and that you truly see the beauty even when it looked like dad was done. God sustained us and grew us and I'm so proud of the men and women of God you've become. I don't deserve such amazing offspring as you all. You bless my life so much.

To my parents, Thomas and Evlyn, Thanks for making me! And thanks for always being there to pick up the pieces and make me feel like I will see better days. For living so faithfully when you walked through the valley seasons, showing me I could make it too.

To my ministry brothers, "the posse," Iron truly sharpens iron and I'm grateful for each of my brothers who have supported me in the valley seasons. You endured many "venting" sessions and you saw me at my real, raw, and most vulnerable moments and yet you loved and encouraged me, spoke truth to me, and even made fun of me which I needed. You kept me humble and focused and pushed me to write this book.

To Joe Bridger and John and Melissa Tillman for helping me sound smarter than I am.

# table of contents

# why this book

This book was inspired by a season of learning God took me through. It was during this season of walking in and through the valley that I realized there is amazing beauty in the valley. Sometimes I've found that the valleys can be even more beautiful than up on the mountaintops.

This book is written to come alongside anyone who leads people but especially those who serve in the church and want to better understand a challenging season that every leader will encounter. It is a season I have named "the valley."

The valley isn't just a season when bad things happen, like depression, unemployment, or failure. Valleys are often most identified as seasons of transition or where things have shifted. What is important to keep in mind is that valleys can be a time when you encounter God in a new way and gain a better understanding of his calling and plan for you.

The valley is a time to be taught by the Holy Spirit. It can be a time of healing, recreation, restoration, and renewal, as well as a time to repair and replace wrong thinking or attitudes for a whole new kind of season.

God uses the time in the valley to get you to look up and to encounter him and understand who he designed you to be. The valley is a time to learn from hurts and failures and to clarify our ideas of success. God wants to prepare you for your next season.

Valleys give you time to process why you're here. In the valley you learn to see what God desires you to be. I encourage you to take your time in valleys and not rush. This is especially true if you have come out of a hurtful situation or find yourself in a place of burnout.

Take it from someone who has been in the valley. You don't want to just put a Band-aid on your wound and then rush to another position. You also can't put out the fire of burnout until you deal with what puts you in the flames. There is no role, or amount of money you could make in that role, that's worth opening another wound. When you do, you risk causing damage to others or yourself.

I encourage you to let God take you to a green pasture in the valley and minister to your spirit. Don't rush this. Instead, embrace it.

I heard a pastor share this verse from the Message and it shook me.

> Here's what I want you to do: Find a quiet, secluded place so you won't be tempted to role-play before God. Just be there as simply and honestly as you can manage. The focus will shift from you to God, and you will begin to sense his grace. -Matthew 6:6 The Message Bible

I love the phrasing of this verse, it really does reflect God's heart for us.

On your journey, I hope you will follow the instructions I've pulled from that passage:

- Find a quiet place.
- Leave the temptation to "be somebody" before God.
- Be present, simple, and honest.
- Allow your heart to shift from focusing on you and your current situation to your Father.
- Keep your heart's gaze directly on him, and then you will experience his amazing grace.

In the valley, there are amazing lessons to be learned. There are lessons from the still and quiet. There are lessons from the loud roar of the river of life rushing around you. There are lessons from the intense darkness where you wonder if you'll ever see the sun (son) again. There are lessons from loneliness. There will be lessons from others who will journey beside you.

All these lessons are valuable and need to be embraced in this season of journeying in the valley.

I pray that, while you read this book, you allow me the honor of being one who walks beside you and that you will also invite the Holy Spirit to walk with us as you read.

We will take our time. We will pause by the stream to reflect. We will worship our amazing God. We will breathe, pray, and cry out to him.

But above all don't leave this valley season until HE calls you out of it.

To all my Kidmin friends. Thanks for cheering me on during this process, I wrote this for you and so many others who serve the Kingdom! God bless your journey!

# chapter one
# THE FIRST VALLEY EXPERIENCE

In the valley, it's quieter. The valley is where you can be alone. When you're alone, especially if you are a people person like me, you will become very lonely. It can be very intense and overwhelming for some. Even the most introverted people don't enjoy loneliness. And in the valley, eventually we all come to a place where we feel very alone and isolated.

Our feelings tell us we are the only ones who care about what we do and how we do it. Our feelings will tell us we are the only ones who can do what we do. Our feelings tell us that if we were gone, no one would even notice. These voices may get loud in your head. It may seem they are telling you the truth and that nothing will ever change. You may feel like Elijah the prophet, saying, "Hey, I'm the only one left, Lord. I'm sitting here in this cave, and it's just miserable. What is wrong with me?"

Remember when Elijah did this in 1 Kings 19? He went to Mount Horeb and went into a cave and there he had a very emotional valley experience at the base of the mountain. It had to have been intense. He was feeling isolated and powerless.

Have you been there, in that place too? I have! I had been running hard and was feeling all alone in the world. I had come to an emotional "cave" and crawled inside. But then something happened to me in a real, physical valley.

I was out in Yosemite National Park hiking with a bunch of children's pastors. We were on a week-long retreat called the Yosemite Summit. And man, that's where it got real.

We were hiking in the valley and I started looking up at the mountains, thinking to myself, "I'd rather be up there. The view has got to be better."

That's when God stopped me in my tracks and spoke to my heart and asked me,

# VALLEYS OVER MOUNTAINS

"When are you going to look around? Look at what I've created down here in the valley. You need to embrace the valley."

I understood, the Spirit wasn't talking about the physical valley I was standing in but the season of life I was now in. I was living and leading on empty. I was at a very low point. The beauty of the location wasn't lost on me and neither was God's voice.

For me it was a 1 Kings 19:9 moment: "There he went into a cave and spent the night. And the word of the Lord came to him: "What are you doing here, Elijah?"

My response was less than enthusiastic. Like Elijah, I was full of excuses and reasons why I didn't want to be there or shouldn't be there. I said, "I know. But this valley stinks. It's a bunch of boring rocks. This valley feels like it is endless. There's nothing down here. I want to get up so I can see the waterfalls again and the mountain peaks, the snow and all the beauty up there."

And God said, "No, no, stay down here and take a look around you. Embrace it!"

That was hard for me. I didn't want to embrace being alone. I feared solitude. I'm a people person, but God wanted me in the valley alone so I could hear him speak.

Solitude is not something everyone enjoys. But after studying how God used solitude in Elijah's and Moses' lives, I began to realize it was a practice I needed to develop.

Solitude is not just sitting alone in a dark room with music and incense. That is the stereotype, but that isn't the correct picture of what it is. Solitude is a powerful practice that can help the valley season become a beautiful place. It's truly a practice of the heart and mind more than being in a certain place. And Solitude is best when your heart is focused on one thing, Jesus.

*Solitude is being alone in order to be with God. Imagine being in a room with a loved one and watching television while other people carry on conversations. If you want to enjoy being together and have a personal conversation of any depth, you have to get up and leave the room. When we choose solitude for quiet time, we are choosing to leave the room to be with*

# THE FIRST VALLEY EXPERIENCE

*our loved One. When we are alone, we can discern God's presence.*

*Martin Luther wrote, "I do not know it and do not understand it, but sounding from above ringing in my ears I hear what is beyond the thought of Man."*

*As I sit in solitude, I frequently find that inner fullness that wells up from inside and pulls me into a deep sense of communion with God. -Stephen Eyre, Drawing Close to God*

There was no place to hide while walking that valley trail. I had to think about myself, my leadership, my team, my dreams, my ministry...everything. It all opened up on that day. Nothing is off limits when Jesus begins to walk beside you.

Let me give you some vulnerable background information. I was serving in a church that was moving fast. I had seen a lot of amazing growth in the ministry I was leading. Many changes had taken place and people were coming to church and joining teams. I was enjoying every part of it. EXCEPT, behind the scenes life was hard.

The staff was not unified. The senior leaders were at odds. I was unfortunately often caught in the middle. I began to isolate and tried to focus only on my ministry area but the enemy knew I was vulnerable and hit me hard. I became discouraged, frustrated, angry, and disrespectful. I resented one of the senior leaders and felt mistreated (in some ways I was). But I let my heart get hard. I had let many little things become bigger, in part because I was a conflict avoider. I had believed the lies the enemy was feeding me but in that valley season I began to gain clarity on how much damage that had caused.

I began to discover in that valley how God wanted me to take care of the hurt and pain I was wrestling with. He wanted me to return to a place of serving him out of love and joy. He wanted me to love that senior leader, no matter what. The valley would become a school. But I had to open my heart and embrace it.

My first valley experience was one I will never ever forget. And I don't want to. I want to remember every moment. I gained so much more wisdom and understanding while in the valley. I want to remember the lessons learned and how I learned them. That's another reason for me to write this. I don't want to forget these lessons and I want to continue to learn from them.

My first valley experience wouldn't be my last valley experience. I've been back a couple of times, but each time I grow more in wisdom, knowledge, and pure understanding. I learn more about myself, my calling and the one who called me.

I'm so grateful that I've learned more about staying in a place where I retained those lessons and that I can safely go back and relearn or gain new insight from looking back. God is so good like that. He wants us to move forward and to learn and grow in a way that fits who he created us to be.

I know when I experience the valley, I have a range of emotions, thoughts, experiences, and you will too. You may ask yourself: Where is God? When will the hurt stop? How long will I feel this constant exhaustion and burn-out? When will a new ministry door open?

But, on the flipside, you may have a sense of peace, relief, joy and such hope that you can hardly express it. That's one thing I've learned about valley experiences; they are never the same. Each one is a unique experience for our good. That's why I think they are beautiful. I don't look back at my experiences in valleys with disdain, I look back and see the growth and wisdom each brought.

Sure there were hard times and many times I didn't enjoy the fact I was there but I learned to trust that God has a plan for me in the valleys. I hang on to that one thing. It keeps my heart pointed in the right direction.

That's why I have come to say, "I think valleys are better than mountaintops." I know it can be hard and challenging but every valley season has been valuable to making me who I am. I now feel better equipped to walk alongside other leaders and guide them through the valleys. When you're walking into the unknown, sometimes you have to do it by yourself and sometimes God brings a guide into your life so that they can help us navigate the trail and help you when you get stuck or find yourself a little lost.

But how do we embrace something that is so hard? How do you embrace something that can be painful or make you feel too vulnerable? What does it mean to actually embrace it? What does it look like? We'll look at that in the next section. For now, pause by this stream and sit a while.

> *"If you think God has forgotten you, then you have forgotten who God is."*
> *-Anonymous*

# pause by the stream

Have you allowed yourself to become vulnerable to the Spirit?

_____

_____

_____

_____

What do you realize has been holding you back from these things? OR what could hold you back?

_____

_____

_____

_____

Is there something you need to let go of so you can walk unhindered?

_____

_____

_____

_____

What Scripture do you need to meditate more on?

_____

_____

_____

_____

# chapter two
# HOW TO PREPARE YOURSELF FOR THE VALLEY

What does it look like to actually enter the valley?

First and foremost, seek to see things with greater clarity.

When you're in that valley moment and you realize that God has a reason for you being down there and he's going to use this for your good, you need to stop and praise him for the realization that you are where you are for a reason. Invite him to show you his purpose. Stop and open your mind and heart to receive.

> *"So humble yourselves under the mighty power of God and at the right time he will lift you up in honor." -1 Peter 5:6 NLT*

Seeking clarity is important to embracing the valley, I find that when I'm in the valley and I am seeking clarity and wisdom I must dig into the Word of God first.

> *"If any of you lacks wisdom, he should ask God, who gives generously to all without finding fault, and it will be given to him." -James 1:5 NIV*

God's Word tells me when I don't see clearly, when I lack understanding and wisdom, that I am to ask him and believe that he will clarify what I cannot see clearly. So while walking through these times we must not ignore the fact it takes time and sometimes it takes leaning into God's Word for wisdom and understanding.

So take a breath and spend some time seeking God. Ask directly and specifically for him to clear your vision so that you can see what the valley looks like. Ask to be able to see what you need to embrace while here.

The second thing upon entering into a valley experience is to stop and check your heart.

# VALLEYS OVER MOUNTAINS

When I was climbing along this trail called the Panorama Trail, it had a series of what are called "switchbacks." These are a series of turns where you walk in a zig-zag pattern rather than going straight up the mountain. Trust me, you don't want to take the straight up route. Your heart will explode! I fell in love with switchbacks. They allowed me to walk to a turn and stop and check my pulse. I was able to control my breathing better at high altitude and catch my breath back so I could continue up the mountain.

When we stop and do a heart check we can then be more receptive to what God desires to teach us during this time.

 I love how tenderly God's Spirit spoke to my heart as I walked through the trails stumbling every once in a while on a stone that had fallen from the face of the mountain. I began to see the object lesson in front of me. The hardness of my heart was keeping me stumbling around instead of walking smoothly and avoiding pain from hitting my foot on a stone.

I had to yield my pride and sinfulness to the Father and allow forgiveness to wash me. It reminded me of God's words to Israel.

> *"I will give you a new heart and put a new spirit in you; I will remove from you your heart of stone and give you a heart of flesh. And I will put my Spirit in you and move you to follow my decrees and be careful to keep my laws."*
> *-Ezekiel 36:26 NIV*

We need a new heart during the valley times. We need to acknowledge the fact that we often default to our own talents and abilities to make things happen. We rely on others' creations and thoughts without really seeking God's wisdom and understanding about what our ministry needs. When that happens we gradually become hardened to the Holy Spirit and his prompts for where and how ministry should happen. Many times I realized that my self-sufficient heart was part of the reason I was so burned out. I was running at my own unhealthy, totally unsustainable pace. I wasn't following the biblical pattern of work. I was pushing myself beyond what God was asking of me.

We can often miss divine appointments where we could have the joy of sharing Jesus with someone because we are so driven by what we want to do and accomplish. So in the valley, we must allow God to do heart surgery on us. I used this scripture while in my valley experience as a daily prayer:

> *Create in me a pure heart, O God, and renew a steadfast spirit within me.*
> *Do not cast me from your presence or take your Holy Spirit from me. Restore*
> *to me the joy of your salvation and grant me a willing spirit, to sustain me.*
> *-Psalm 51:10 NIV*

Restoring a heart is the second step into the valley.

A third  area that God taught me about while in the valley is embracing vulnerability. You must become vulnerable. This means you must allow yourself to be open to whatever the Spirit is working on in your life and how it will serve a greater purpose in the next season.

*I want to talk more about seasons with you, but that will be a different section.*

Becoming totally vulnerable to the Spirit means that, as you take a step down the path you say, "Okay God. I want you to recreate me! I want to lean into you during this valley time. I want you to speak loud and clear." But you may not hear the load roaring thunder or see a burning bush. God loves to speak in that still small voice.  Elijah experienced this kind of quiet voice of God for himself in one of his valley times.

What must that have been like? The Hebrew we translate as "still small voice" can mean "the sound of silence." What is that? What does silence sound like? Whatever it sounds like, it drew Elijah out.  His feelings must have been so vulnerable and exposed at that moment that Scripture, in 1 Kings 19:13, says he covered his face and came out of the cave.

When you are in the valley,  and become vulnerable enough,  God can call you out and speak life to you in the silence. He can clarify his dream for you, what you are to continue to do, start to do,  or even stop doing. When you are vulnerable you just want someone to provide you that clear path to take another step. God asked Elijah again, "What are you doing here, Elijah?"

Elijah expressed his vulnerable state and fear and then God said, "Go back the way you came and go…" He sent him on his new mission. He also sent him to find a helper and, eventually, the one he was to mentor to be his replacement.

## VALLEYS OVER MOUNTAINS

Being vulnerable lets you listen to God and allows God time to speak. God wasn't done with Elijah in the cave and he wasn't done teaching me lessons to embrace my valley season.

Our final lesson on entering the valley is something really personal to me.

While I was on this walk of solitude, I realized that I was carrying around a lot of negative emotions, feelings, and attitudes that God didn't want me to carry. I had been doing most of my ministry in my own power instead of his. I wanted to be the center of the ministry. I was also more concerned about what people thought of me than what he thought of me. I had an approval addiction. I wanted to find my worth in what people saw in me and what I did. God saw through my "performance." He knew my motivation wasn't where it should be.

Since God wanted me to see the beauty in where I was, I started looking around. I saw flowers and greenery. I saw things growing in amazing ways. I saw this little tree growing right out of a rock.

## HOW TO PREPARE YOURSELF FOR THE VALLEY

The picture was again becoming more clear to me. Ministry can be really hard and really draining down in the valley. The reality is you will get knocked over sometimes but, if your roots are deep and solid in the rock, you can survive and thrive. But choose to carry around the negative things I mentioned above and your roots will not be solid.

So the choice is yours, you can let go of what you're carrying around and allow God to work in you to deepen your roots, or you can resist.

It always amazes me where growth can happen in my life. When I look back, it is often in the valley times, where I have grown the most. Valleys are truly beautiful places.

Think of Psalm 1 where David describes a "blessed" man as one who is like a tree. Soak in this for a moment and let your roots go down into this passage.

> *Blessed is the man*
> *who does not walk in the counsel of the wicked*
> *or stand in the way of sinners*
> *or sit in the seat of mockers.*
> *But his delight is in the law of the Lord,*
> *and on his law he meditates day and night.*
> *He is like a tree planted by streams of water,*
> *which yields its fruit in season*
> *and whose leaf does not wither.*
> *Whatever he does prospers.*
> *-Psalm 1 NIV*

When you are in a valley you need to take a long hard look at your root system and how deep it goes. What are you allowing into your life that affects those roots and the fruit you want to bear? The key to a good root system is in the middle of this scripture: *but his delight is in the law of the LORD, and on his law he meditates day and night.*

Want deep strong roots? Delight (fall deeper in love with) God's Word and do all you can to follow in obedience no matter what culture tells you. Dig into it so hard that you are "meditating" on it all day. It's what you think about. It's better than binge watching anything online. When you're deeply rooted, even when the "rockslides" happen you will be ok.

Take a look at different scriptures that remind us just how powerful meditating on God's Word is:

I have more insight than all my teachers, for I meditate on your statutes. Psalm 119:99 NIV

> *May the words of my mouth and the meditation of my heart be pleasing in your sight, O Lord, my Rock and my Redeemer. -Psalm 19:14 NIV*

# pause by the stream

Have you allowed yourself to become vulnerable to the Spirit?

_____

_____

_____

_____

What do you realize has been holding you back from these things? OR what could hold you back?

_____

_____

_____

_____

Is there something you need to let go of so you can walk unhindered?

_____

_____

_____

_____

What Scripture do you need to meditate more on?

_____

_____

_____

_____

# chapter three
# EMBRACE THE VALLEY

*When you find yourself in a valley season you must learn to not resist, but to embrace it. Don't rush your way through. Embrace it fully, in total surrender.*
*-Tom*

When you begin to realize you are entering a valley season, whether it's because of a job change, a spiritual dry season, or from running so hard you've worn yourself down, you will need to learn something very quickly. You must learn to embrace the valley. As you do this it will lead you to ask many questions.

I've been in full time ministry since the age of nineteen, and I've come to learn that even after just a few years, you may find yourself in a valley experience. It is in these times you need to stop and ask God, "Why am I here?"

There were many times in ministry where I hit THE SPOT! I was operating in my gifting! I was in the zone! I knew God called me to that moment of ministry. But then I hit a wall and I knew something was wrong. I started to pull back from my family and my ministry team. I started to isolate myself from everyone and everything.

Things got quieter, I wasn't laughing as much. The joy of serving and leading wasn't there. I was in "copy and paste" mode. I did a lot of comparing my ministry to others. The Internet and conferences I attended weren't sources of inspiration or joy but opportunities to play the comparison game and to find stuff to copy and paste into my work. I would search for things I could plug and play instead of being inventive and seeking God for his creativity and his resources. I was just content with the old easy way of doing ministry. I said to myself, "Hey, this has always worked for me. Let's just do it this way because it'll get me by. I'll just grind it out." Fake it till you make it, right?

Ever been there?

# VALLEYS OVER MOUNTAINS

Instead of asking the right questions I went after my own solutions, and that NEVER worked. I became very resistant to being down in the valley. I was in places where I wasn't seeing a lot of ministry growth. What I didn't realize was that my team wasn't growing because I wasn't growing as a leader. Eventually, I realized that God was using those valley experiences to grow me like that little tree growing in the rock.

God uses valley times to refine and renew us. We sometimes don't think we need refinement or renewal. Sometimes we don't feel tired or worn out. But this isn't just about how we physically feel. We also need emotional and mental refinement and renewal. In the valley, God exposes these areas to us and shows us the blind spots in our lives. There is so much to consider once the realization becomes clear that you are in a valley season.

The best part of being in the valley though, is to know that God is at work in you and that he is giving you the opportunity to see him work. As you draw closer to him during this valley season, you will be amazed at what the Spirit shows you. But you must be ready to receive and accept the fact you are here for a special reason and purpose. You must learn to embrace it. Don't be discouraged by this season, that is what the enemy wants for you.

As you learn to embrace the valley, you will have to put on God's armor.

> Finally, be strong in the Lord and in his mighty power. Put on the full armor of God so that you can take your stand against the devil's schemes. -Ephesians 6:10, NIV

All scripture tells us to do is "stand" in God's armor. It is God who will fight for us." It is his armour that protects and provides the safety we need while in the valley. It is his strength we stand in, walk in, and grow in.

Valley experiences are not always when your ministry is failing. They can also be times where you are seeing plateaus or times where things are going well but happening on cruise control. It's a place where you see good things happening, but you know there is something better out there that you just don't see clearly yet.

During a past ministry season, I asked God, "what do you want me to learn?"

# EMBRACE THE VALLEY

The ministry was growing nicely, teams were happy and healthy on the surface, and I was basically enjoying what I was doing. It was smooth. It was controlled... cruise controlled. I didn't want people to think I was unhappy or frustrated. The more I hid my feelings and kept working, the worse the feeling got. I was frustrated with being in the valley.

If you want to benefit and grow from a valley season, you need to have a learner's heart and attitude. God will have lessons around every curve and over the next hilltop.

One of the lessons I learned was that I wasn't leaning into the Spirit for help since I felt that I had it under control. I also felt like I was in a safe place and didn't want to rock the boat. Then I had a friend question me. He asked, if I felt like I was doing all I could to lead more to reach more?

The answer was, honestly, no. I hadn't built a team around me to help grow the ministry. I wasn't leading others to use their gifts and talents to reach more with the gospel. But why add more when I finally had everything going? I worked so hard, sacrificed so much to get to this place, why change?

I felt like I didn't need to learn anything new or fresh. It wasn't broken, so why fix it?

His challenge to me was to ask God if there was something more. I didn't want to do that. I knew it was a dangerous question to ask.

I realized I needed to hit a pause button on my life. I chose to step away for a few days and get into nature for some silence and solitude. I needed to "pause by the stream." What I want you to do in this moment, and in subsequent moments to follow, is to pause. Imagine yourself sitting by a stream in the middle of the woods. It's lush and green. It's quiet and tranquil yet filled with the music of nature, except for the buzzing bugs. But if you're inside, using your imagination, it's bug free! Take some time to create some mental space in your head and heart where you can be still and quiet before the Lord.

*Be Still and KNOW, I AM God. -Psalm 46:10a, NIV*

You cannot rush through a valley season and then say to God, "Ok, I'm done, call me up!" We don't do that. It doesn't work. You can try, I guess. I did. But you'll find you're going to walk the valley as long as you need to. God's timing is never our timing, but like an old song says, "he's always right on time." So you might as well relax and embrace this season. That's the reason for the "Pause by the Stream" to help you stop, and reflect. Consider what you are learning, not from my simple words, but from what God is teaching you. For me the process of getting healthy and moving out of valley seasons took time. One trip won't be the same as others. Your experiences won't be the same if you come back to a valley. But I am confident in what I'm telling you and what I've told others whom I've coached in this process. If you don't embrace the valley and hit the pause button to learn, the valley will be a lot harder than you want it to be.

The choice is yours. Embrace it or fight it but either way, you're here and you are here for God's purpose. You are here to learn what he wants you to learn, so you might as well embrace it! Here's what I suggest when you come to these sections. Block off one hour. If you can, go to a place where you can have solitude. If you can't, do whatever you have to do to give you some peaceful time to reflect, listen, and hear that still small voice. Try turning off notifications and putting on a white noise app with the sound of running water or whatever relaxes you. Play some instrumental worship, light a candle, whatever works for you. Answer these questions during your pause. Don't let yourself answer too quickly. Sometimes the easy answer isn't the best answer or even the right one. Let the Spirit confirm your answers. Again I'm going to challenge you as you begin this journey to follow Matthew 6:6.

> *Here's what I want you to do: Find a quiet, secluded place so you won't be tempted to role-play before God. Just be there as simply and honestly as you can manage. The focus will shift from you to God, and you will begin to sense his grace. -Matthew 6:6, The Message Bible*

# pause by the stream

Have you been sensing in your spirit that you are spiritually dry?

_____

_____

_____

_____

Have you been operating on "cruise control?"

_____

_____

_____

_____

What do you need to stop and address right now? What are some things that you know are not healthy or in balance?

_____

_____

_____

_____

What do you sense God showing you about what you need to learn?

_____

_____

_____

_____

# VALLEYS OVER MOUNTAINS

What do you believe about putting on God's armor? Look deeper into Ephesians 6 and reflect:

_____

_____

_____

_____

_____

_____

_____

_____

What do you hope is waiting for you on the other side of the valley experiences?

_____

_____

_____

_____

_____

_____

_____

_____

# chapter four
# VALLEYS AREN'T ALWAYS FLAT

I needed a new hill to climb. I discovered one reason I was in the valley was for God to show me that seasons are designed to go up and down, even the "mountaintop" seasons.

When you allow yourself to just stroll along in life and ministry you tend to rely on your own talents and gifts. You repeat what always worked and you never ask, "Is this the best we have?" If this is you, do you need to ask the question my friend challenged me with?

*"God, is there something more you want me to do? Is there something you want me to learn?*

*Is there something new you want me to push for?"*

When I began to pray the previous prayers and then asked, "God what are you preparing me for?" God began to open my heart and mind up to new ideas. These ideas were outside my comfort zone. I also knew that if I wanted to lead more I had to stay in a place where God could prepare me to do so. That meant even longer in the valley, but I learned this isn't a bad thing.

Look at Moses and his time in the wilderness before the burning bush. Check out Exodus chapters three and four.

> *Now Moses was tending the flock of Jethro, his father-in-law, the priest of Midian, and he led the flock to the far side of the desert and came to Horeb, the mountain of God. There the angel of the Lord appeared to him in flames of fire from within a bush. Moses saw that though the bush was on fire it did not burn up. So Moses thought, "I will go over and see this strange sight— why the bush does not burn up."*

> *When the Lord saw that he had gone over to look, God called to him from*

*within the bush, "Moses! Moses!" And Moses said, "Here I am."*

*"Do not come any closer," God said. "Take off your sandals, for the place where you are standing is holy ground." Then he said, "I am the God of your father, the God of Abraham, the God of Isaac and the God of Jacob." At this, Moses hid his face, because he was afraid to look at God.*

God used the valley to get Moses's attention. He had been leading sheep all over the desert and came to Horeb, God's mountain. It was here that God did something to get his attention, he started burning inside of a bush and Moses got curious. *"I will go over and see this strange sight." (vs.3)*

God had his attention and wanted to push him outside of his comfort zone and get him to consider a bigger mission than leading sheep across a dusty desert. When we are in the valley and God starts to do things like this, we should want to see what he's up to. I will testify that this can be one of the scariest things you'll ever do. I'm sure Moses, seeing some bush that appeared to be on fire but wasn't burning up, had to have been just a bit scared. When you begin to ask God to help you see why you are in the valley don't be surprised if he asks you to do something outside of your comfort zone.

When God began to push and pull me, I can admit that I pushed back like Moses and made all sorts of excuses for why I shouldn't go bigger, go better, or go anywhere outside of my comfort zone.

Look at Moses' excuses:

- Who am I? Exodus 3:11
- What if they ask who sent me? Exodus 3:13
- What if they don't believe me or listen to me? Exodus 4:1
- I have never been eloquent  Exodus 4:10
- O Lord, please send someone else to do it. 4:10

Ever say any of those excuses? If you haven't yet, you probably will. And I'm willing to admit I've said all of them. I was in a valley asking God to show me greater things and, when he showed them to me in my heart, I began to offer up lame excuses as to why I couldn't come close to accomplishing them.

# VALLEYS AREN'T ALWAYS FLAT

God understands those moments. While he still got mad at Moses for questioning his power and ability to accomplish the tasks he was calling Moses to, I think it's safe to assume God placed this account in Scripture so that we could learn from it. Hopefully, we won't repeat it and will instead follow him in total obedience. We see the results clearly. Then Moses obeys, God does exactly what he said he would do and uses Moses and Aaron to free people from bondage.

For me, the times I'm in these valleys are times where I see God giving me greater missions. I just want to obey what he has set in front of me. I know by experience, as Moses knew in those days after the bush, that God will do way more than we ask or think!

So let's recap. Moses was in a valley and God used the lessons he learned while leading sheep to eventually lead the Isrealites out of Egypt. It was hard work. God was doing faith-stretching, soul-stretching work in those times. When he was ready, God called Moses up the mountain to that burning bush and spoke a new vision and set a new course for his life.

Moses was in a place to receive but his heart had some resistance. He had been in the schools of the Pharaoh and now he was leading sheep. That in itself is a huge contrast and has lots of ministry lessons. If we want to lead well, we need to work at keeping our hearts in a receiving mode. When our lives are out of balance, we move into a place of resistance.

When we are there, the excuses begin to flow out of our mouths. "This won't work!" "That won't work!" We become cynical and harsh and filled with self-doubt.

I think some of this is seen in Moses' list of excuses and I understand from personal experience. When I was in the valley, God showed me clearly that I had allowed these things to creep into my spirit and instead of being in a place of receiving I was resistant.

One reason I was resistant was fear. I had let the fear of man become larger than the fear of God. It had become not just a hill I had to climb over but a stronghold I needed to break through. I know if you've been in ministry for a while, you have probably climbed a hill like this or at least wrestled with fear of some kind.

I also struggled with a fear of failure. When I failed, I was ashamed and that shame was devastating to me. Also, the shame came from someone I was trying to please all the time so my fear of man made fear of failure an even bigger stronghold. It affected me in so many ways it's scary.

I can remember the first time this monster hit. It was just a few weeks before a Vacation Bible School for my church. I was a bit behind in my planning and had pushed too many things down the road and it caught up to me. Yes, it could have been prevented but it wasn't and I was now waking up in the middle of the night in a full blown panic attack.

I felt like I was having a heart attack. I got up out of bed and went into our small bathroom and began to pray. I cried out to God for peace. I checked my pulse. It was ok, but I couldn't catch my breath and wound up laying on the floor. I was so overcome with fear because I knew if this event didn't attract enough kids like it did in the past, I would be criticized. The Senior Pastor made it very clear my job could be in jeopardy if I didn't start producing bigger numbers at these keystone events. My fear of man and fear of failure combined for a double whammy that night.

I also experienced a time where the reason I was resistant is because there were things in my life that were sinful. A hill I had to climb over in that case was my own anger.

I'll be sharing many stories from my own experience later, but for now let me pause in this space and address some of these smaller hills where we often resist God's Spirit and we push back instead of pushing through. Anger is one of those hills.

> In your anger do not sin": Do not let the sun go down while you are still angry, and do not give the devil a foothold. -Ephesians 4:26-27, NIV

As leaders, we often dismiss our anger and try to bury it deep inside of us as we don't want to come across to anyone as unkind or unloving. Anger can really hurt us, and yet, we allow our anger to burn quietly inside of us. This is so dangerous! Do you see what Paul writes in verse 27? Do NOT give the devil a FOOTHOLD! This means when we hold onto anger in our lives we literally give the enemy a place to stand in our lives. When we are in the valley and crossing over a hill anger sometimes comes out and we see it. It's ugly. It burns, it wounds, it hurts others and ourselves, and it allows the enemy a place to attack us from.

We can be encouraged by what Jesus said in John 14:30, *"I will not speak with you much longer, for the prince of this world is coming. He has no hold on me."* (NIV)

Addressing our anger in life during the valley times allows us to better deal with it when we are on the mountain. God had to address my anger in the valley by having me pause by a raging river to show me its power. Have you ever sat by a river that is full from the mountain snowmelt?

Let me tell you, it's loud, wild, foamy, intense, and scary. Our anger is the same. I found that I had pushed anger under the surface. Even when others had hurt me deeply, or when I felt used by someone, I'd quickly brush it off and say, "I'm ok, we're fine." The truth was, I would have loved to shove them into the raging river.

Addressing anger is a process. As a part of that process, I encourage you to do a word study on the word anger. I'll only take a look at one more verse with you and trust you to do the rest.

> For man's anger does not bring about the righteous life that God desires.
> -James 1:20, NIV

When we don't dig into who we are angry with, why we are angry, and how to manage it, we miss out on the life God intends for us to live and we cannot lead with the effectiveness he desires us to lead with.

While in this valley, take a look and see if you are struggling with anger that's been buried for a while. Ask God to show you what it is and as you dig into his Word about it, ask that you would experience forgiveness and offer forgiveness to those whom you need to forgive.

These are the hills you climb over when in the valley. Some are steep, some are a gentle climb, but they are ones you must walk your way over and not around. You must take a deep look inside and see what has gotten in the way of your clear view of the path you should be walking when walking in obedience. The Great I AM wants to show you that he keeps his promises. The Great I AM wants to show you he has the power to break down strongholds in your life. The Great I AM can take your excuses and give you promises to cling to as you take your steps up the mountain where he wants to show you even more. Are you ready to receive? What are some of the "hills" you are facing? Don't try to take the shortcut around them. Part of embracing this whole process is facing those hills and climbing them. When you do, you'll realize they are part of the beauty of the valley.

# pause by the stream

Take a moment to think about where you are in your personal, spiritual relationship with God? Are you in a place of receiving or resistance?

_____

_____

_____

If you're in a place of resistance, why do you think you're resisting?

_____

_____

_____

_____

What excuses do you struggle with when you think about what may be next for you?

_____

_____

_____

_____

Why do you think you are in the valley? It's ok to not understand it yet.

_____

_____

_____

_____

# VALLEYS OVER MOUNTAINS

Is your heart really open to what God is showing you? If you can't see or sense anything, stop and ask the Father to gently open your heart, eyes, and ears.

When it comes to anger, how do you handle it?

_____

_____

_____

_____

Is there some unresolved anger in your life? What steps should you take to resolve it?

_____

_____

_____

_____

# chapter five
# VALLEYS CAN BE MESSY

Ministry is hard. I know you get it, right? When you are leading people who are broken and you yourself are broken, things are bound to wind up like a rockslide sometimes.

When you are in the valley, sometimes you have to figure out how to navigate your own life amidst all the falling stones that are happening as messy ministry continues. The valley is a place where rockslides happen and you can either be in the right place or the wrong place when they happen. When you are walking in the valley, you are more vulnerable to falling rocks. But trust me, when time passes you find beauty even in rockslides.

I've learned over the years that sometimes, in the messiest of times, beauty emerges both in me and in those around me. Sounds a lot like the principles from Rom. 8:28 again, right? God truly works in and through the messes.

The area I was hiking in had seen a terrible rockslide. I've seen some videos of rockslides happening. They are terrifying! That was why I was always looking up at the canyon walls. I was a bit nervous about being in the wrong place at the wrong time. When we are in the ministry valley we should always be paying attention to our surroundings. We sometimes don't maintain our personal lives that well and, when we don't, it can become a mess internally.

One example is how sometimes we value work over family even though we'd never admit to that. (Out loud anyway.) This can make us vulnerable to a personal rockslide. It is sad to see. I've seen it happen to some of my ministry friends. I've watched marriages that, looking from outside, were seemingly healthy, but began to crack and crumble.

My friends, please. I beg of you to be real in the valley. If you are married, please be married to your spouse and not the church even if it costs you your job. If a church ever asks more of you than you can truly give, get out. If you are a Senior Leader, please don't demand you or your staff jeopardize marriages for the sake of the ministry. This doesn't make sense, is not biblical, and is a terrible example to the world.

We shouldn't be bragging that we spend more time in church than we do with our families and we shouldn't believe the lie that just because our families are serving with us that that justifies more time in the ministry.

And that's just one example. Let's move on.

While hiking through the rockslide area, I was amazed that even in devastation there was amazing beauty. There was a new path created. The scenery changed, but the destination was still the same.

When we walk the valleys, even when our lives and ministries get messy, we can still arrive where God desires us to be, but only if we do it the right way. When we force the rockslide to happen, it will have tremendous effects on everything and everyone around us. Just look at that picture of the rockslide. The nature around that place was entirely changed because of one rockslide. Everything was impacted. Everything.

In the messiness of the valley, I feel like I went through a couple of stages. You will probably experience similar stages.

One was realizing how broken and fragile I was. I believe this is why 2 Corinthians tells us this:

> But we have this treasure in jars of clay to show that this all-surpassing power is from God and not from us. We are hard pressed on every side, but not crushed; perplexed, but not in despair; persecuted, but not abandoned; struck down, but not destroyed. -2 Corinthians 4:7-9, NIV

In ministry during the valley season, we can come to realize that we may feel totally broken and useless but if you read this verse, we are "hard pressed" but NOT <u>crushed</u>! You may feel totally destroyed or broken right now, but this verse tells us that we are not crushed, destroyed, or abandoned.

The time in the valley helps you gain perspective that you sometimes don't have on top of the mountain. It takes time to realize the lies we have come to embrace or personalize. But the valley can help us see them more clearly. That's a good thing. If you want to get healthy, if you want to gain wisdom in the valley, embrace this and let the Spirit show you your pride, arrogance, and overconfidence or your self-pity, doubt, and lack of confidence. These things will keep you in the wrong place and will truly overwhelm you. Eventually they could destroy your influence, reputation, and ministry.

Another stage that I feel like I went through while in the valley was coming to a place of true repentance from how I had been living and serving. I had become complacent, prideful, and reliant on cruise control. I lived for the praise of men and enjoyed it when I got a few accolades. I did so much to have people notice me. I see it sometimes in others now too. My heart aches for some in ministry who build their platforms and followings. They push themselves in front of the ministry world because they want to be known and appreciated.

While in the valley this was so much of what I had to repent of. I needed to turn from seeking what the world thought was success and toward what matters to God. For me, early on in ministry, I had a strong dream to be speaking. I wanted to be on larger ministry conference stages. I wanted to be a breakout speaker. I wanted to be what we often consider "ministry famous." What is ministry famous? In ministry circles there are certain people who get invited to every conference, podcast, etc. They are treated like celebrities.

I wanted to be noticed, I wanted the praise or acknowledgement of people. I was always comparing myself to others who were getting the attention. I wanted the "likes" and "follows." I'm not criticising those who have achieved this, or who get recognized as someone to follow in ministry.

But I had to confess that I was pursuing the wrong things and I need to fully turn away from that. My heart's desire and the pursuit of the season of life I'm in now is about Kingdom work, not my work. All I want to do is get up every day and stand clean before my heavenly father. I want to be motivated by what is pure and holy and I want God to provide the opportunities for me to serve, not my manufacturing of them. If, someday, I get a high profile invite, I will humbly accept it, but it will be God opening the door, not me kicking it in.

I hope and pray this makes sense. I hope it helps you take a deeper look inside yourself and say, are there goals, motivations, pursuits, desires, that need to be laid on the altar and repented from?

# VALLEYS CAN BE MESSY

I think the final stage for me was to take all the messiness and choose and declare that I would leave this in the valley and not pick it back up. The treasure we get to carry and represent while serving God is completed because of who he is and his power in us. We have to carry it with completely open hands. It's not ours to grasp, build, or take. We don't get to dictate how it's used. This gospel is HIS!

As I've come to embrace this I realize how much I still struggle with it. Do you still play the comparison game? It's when you look at what everyone else is doing and you compare what you have in your hands to what others are carrying in their hands.

I have to realize that if I grip too tightly to this "clay pot" I can let it squeeze out of my hands or I won't be able to receive anything else. If I carry it open handed, willing to set it down or pick it up when I'm asked to, it is a better way to live.

Some who know me wonder why I love to do so many different things in ministry. I've been told I should focus on one thing or I'll never be good at anything. I don't buy it. I truly believe that if I'm living in God's truth and power and I'm staying spiritually filled and where he desires me to be I can carry multiple pots and use them all for his glory alone. Consider Colossians 3:17:

> And whatever you do, whether in word or deed, do it all in the name of the Lord Jesus, giving thanks to God the Father through him. NIV

What has gotten messy in your world? Have you lost sight of why you started in ministry? Have you been caught up in the comparison game? We must keep as our North Star the remembrance that everything we do, EVERYTHING, is done in his name and for his glory alone.

Maybe in this valley season, you are here to get reacquainted with your true focus and calling and get ready for the next season. Maybe you're here because you need to let go, give away, or repent of those weights that keep you from doing what God has called you to.

It takes time and being open to see these things and it can hurt. When I walked through these things I didn't want to believe I had been guilty of them. But God confirmed them in me and I wasn't going to argue with my maker. Instead, I took the time to repent. I want to live in a way where I can guard myself against ever going back to that way of life.

I may struggle at times with some of these things, but they do not have the stronghold in my life that they used to have. I am much more sensitive to when the comparison demon shows up to whisper in my ear. I can't hear him when the helmet of salvation is on anyway!

Take some time to pause and rest. Take some time to reflect here for a while. Don't be in a rush to move through the process. Embrace the mess and know he's ready to forgive and guide you back to the path he has chosen for you to walk.

**Sit and meditate on these scriptures as you prepare to pause by the stream again:**

*O Lord, you have searched me and you know me. You know when I sit and when I rise; you perceive my thoughts from afar. You discern my going out and my lying down; you are familiar with all my ways. -Psalm 139:1-3, NIV*

*Search me, O God, and know my heart; test me and know my anxious thoughts. See if there is any offensive way in me, and lead me in the way everlasting. -Psalm 139:23-24, NIV*

# pause by the stream

Where are you vulnerable to a rockslide spiritually, emotionally, physically, relationally?

_____

_____

_____

_____

Is there something in your life that, if it got messier, would cause a rockslide?

_____

_____

What do you need to change to prevent a rockslide in your life?

_____

_____

_____

_____

Reflect a while on Psalm 1- How deep are your roots? What can you do to improve your own delight in God's Word? Do you have scheduled time to dig deeper and meditate on the Word?

_____

_____

_____

_____

# VALLEYS OVER MOUNTAINS

Are there some strongholds in your life that shouldn't be there? What are they?

_____

_____

_____

_____

Have you allowed yourself to lose focus on what your calling is? Where did it change?

_____

_____

_____

_____

_____

_____

What are the steps you need to take to get your hands open and your heart right?

_____

_____

_____

_____

# chapter six
# DON'T IGNORE THE "WHY" OF THE VALLEY

I've served in nearly every role around the church. I've been a volunteer, full time children's pastor, student pastor, and even a senior pastor for a little while. And, in any role, you can experience an emotional dryness, a season where you're going through the motions and you're not seeing a fresh wind and a fresh fire blowing through anything you're doing.

*The old saying is true: If you have only the Word, you dry up.*
*If you have only the Spirit, you blow up.*
*But if you have both, you grow up.*
**-Jim Cymbala, Fresh Wind, Fresh Fire**

Many leaders believe they can keep going and going and they don't need to stop and talk about valley experiences. I made that mistake. You need to stop and look around the valley. You need to hit an emotional pause button and seek out the answers God wants to show you at this time.

Leaders can show up faking it for many weekends. I know what this is like, as I became a master at it, putting a smile on my face, grinding through, hinking, "I'll just push through and then I'll get a vacation." But vacations don't seem to refresh and renew..

I saw other leaders burning up and out. I saw leaders who looked like they had everything together  take their own lives because of anxiety, depression, etc. The valley became too dark and overwhelming for them.

Emotional lows can be dangerous if we don't seek out help. I am a firm believer that we need to stand guard regarding  our emotions. We need to make sure we never think they can't get the best of us.

We have seen some high profile leaders who have ended their own lives because they were spent emotionally. They hit such a low that the pain became too great to hide anymore and they stopped living. When these stories hit the news, they hit those of us in ministry so hard. I am thankful for a group of people in my life who cared enough to actually reach out to make sure I was ok. I did that for some of my ministry friends as well.

Hear me when I say, "if you are in ministry, you are vulnerable." Don't ever say that it won't or can't happen to me. The enemy is vicious and, in a season of emotional dryness, it can happen to anyone. We must stand guard for each other and we must be humble enough to admit when we need help and accountability.

Professional counseling and sometimes medication are tools that God has provided to help us and we should use them. I went to counseling as I realized I was in a dangerous emotional place and I needed help to get out. God helped me to realize that there was not a way to pray myself out. I couldn't program myself out. I couldn't vacation it out.

I needed someone to talk to and someone to help me figure out what the cause was and how to prevent it from happening again.

If you need to see a counselor, realize there is no shame. It is not a sign of weakness or inability to perform your job. I truly believe we in the church have done grave damage to so many servants because we stigmatized going to a counselor for help. Please don't let it stop you. **You are worth it!**

When we are walking in the valley, these are good times to do an emotional intelligence check up. But don't answer questions for yourself. Ask others to answer on your behalf. You will cheat. I did. So will you.

*I discovered an astonishing truth: God is attracted to weakness. He can't resist those who humbly and honestly admit how desperately they need him.*
*Our weakness, in fact, makes room for his power.*
**-Jim Cymbala, Fresh Wind, Fresh Fire**

So when you find yourself in a place of dryness emotionally what can you do? Here are some basic steps I learned.

## DON'T IGNORE THE "WHY" OF THE VALLEY

Ask yourself some of the following questions. I'd also encourage you to connect with another leader you trust who has more ministry experience and ask them these questions:

- What have you read in scripture lately that moved you emotionally?
- What have you seen God do lately?
- What's something new about God you've learned?
- What is your devotional time with God like?
- What is your worship routine like?
- When was the last time you told anyone about something that hurt? Did you address/reconcile/forgive/let go?
- What do you do to pause and physically rest?

I know there are many other things you can ask and that these questions aren't a substitute for a full on counseling session. They will help you become more self aware. This is something all leaders need to improve on. Spiritual/emotional dryness can be a warning and it must be addressed and walked through. When we do, it is a healthy and beautiful process. Yes, it can hurt too, but you will be so much stronger on the other side of it

For me, having a counselor walk me through the deep places of my heart brought healing and health. I needed to walk in that valley and climb those hills so that I can live the way my Creator designed me to live.

I will conclude this section by saying that not everything rises to the level where professional counseling is necessary. I do believe, as Paul in Romans 12 charged us, with renewing our minds. We must in fact daily allow the Spirit of God to renew us. But dealing with your emotional well-being is not a solo sport. You will need help at some point. Consider yourself with sober judgment and don't be overconfident. Err on the side of caution and seek help before it becomes too late.

The mental healing Paul encourages will only happen when we immerse ourselves deeply into the Word and allow it to do what only it can do. When the living word begins to cut into the parts that need spiritual surgery it brings healing and life to those parts that are dying or already dead. It brings moisture to the dry soul.

# VALLEYS OVER MOUNTAINS

Some will wonder and ask, how will I know if I'm in the right place? Read Romans 15:13b and ask yourself, "am I experiencing the overflow of hope by the power of the Holy Spirit?" When your heart is in the right place, you can live out of the overflow of hope again.

If you are going to embrace this valley you must prepare yourself to push through anything and everything God has for you in this place. You may have to overcome some large things in your life, but there will be smaller things that can be just as challenging or painful. Preparing yourself and determining that you will push through no matter what is a resolve that must come from deep down.

For me, the words "push through" carry deep meaning. Many times while hiking I have heard those words in my mind at just the right time, "push through!" There were times on the trail that it was so hard and so steep, I would say out loud, "I don't think I can do this," or "I don't want to do this" and then I'd hear those words; "Push through!"

I remember a time on one trail when we encountered unexpected water that was much deeper than we thought it would be. It was futile to try to find another spot to hike and so we had no choice but to take the boots and socks off and begin walking. That water was soooo cold! I'm talking, it made my bones scream inside my legs cold. I have never desired to stick my legs into a place where it felt like daggers were stabbing me with each step but that's what it was like. It was crazy but we had no choice.

With each step I would tell myself, "push through, " every time it hurt to put a foot down, "push through." The only relief we had were a few high spots or fallen logs where we could step up and get some warmth and more circulation happening. Then we would have to, "push through" and step back into that water because someone else needed that high spot. We had to keep moving, hoping at some point the trail would clear and we would be back on dry ground.

There will be times in this valley season when you will feel that kind of soul ripping pain. I want you to again hear me, on the other side of this is healing. I know, and can testify, that after we walk through and push through what God has for us in seasons like this, we experience the sweet relief and the amazing beauty on the other side. One more "push through" story and then we are going to pause and allow the Spirit to show you where you need to push through.

I was on a final day of hiking and decided to take a little trip to the base of El Capitan which normally is a simple little walk, no hiking boots required. It's a flat, boring path that winds its way to the base of the monstrous wall of granite. I think it's that way because so many of the climbers have to carry in their supplies. The easy path makes that possible.

I chose to walk that path and chose not to wear my hiking boots because it was such a simple thing. I was with two of my friends and we decided we wanted to get up close and personal with this rock by walking to the base. I was excited as I'd taken so many pictures of the famous place.

I'd stared at climbers making their way up the face. I wanted to put my hands on it. I wanted to take some pictures that I only imagined would be amazing from the bottom looking up to the top—over three thousand feet up!

So we began walking. Then I realized that one of my friends, and shortly after both of my friends, had left the trail and were now working their way through the brush to an area where there had been a rockslide many years ago. They were going to take a "shortcut."

## VALLEYS OVER MOUNTAINS

At first, I had no desire to take that shortcut. I wanted the easy path. I also hadn't worn the proper shoes for bouldering. It definitely is not advisable to just climb around on boulders when you only have sneakers on. Those huge chunks of granite are slick and sharp.

But I wanted to keep up so I pushed my way in too.

It didn't take long to realize I had made a huge mistake with the shoes I was wearing. I was slipping and sliding all over. I slid down one side of a boulder only to slide into a sharp edge and... ouch! Yep. The blood began to flow.

It was a much steeper climb than I had anticipated. The boulders were bigger the farther we went. It didn't take long before I lost my friends as they were eagerly moving on. I sat on a rock while I got the bleeding leg cleaned up and proceeded to consider my options.

Keep bouldering up? Or figure out my way off these boulders and back to the easy path.

I wanted to quit. I wanted to stop and go back. It was the easy and probably most logical choice, but who wants to admit that they quit? Not me!

Well, actually yes, part of me was ready to say, "I quit and I don't care who knows it." But, that voice in my head whispered, "push through."

I sat and looked up that cliff and could hear climbers talking. The sun was gleaming off its face. I began to talk to myself (and God) about it. I began to ask, do I really want to keep climbing? Do I really keep pushing through? Would this painful climb be worth it in the end?

You may find yourself asking those same questions as you work your way through this valley season. You may have thought, "I want the easy path!" I'll tell you, "no, you don't. You really don't"

Why don't you want the easy path in a valley season? Let me finish my story for you and then you'll understand.

As I was continuing my conversation with God about whether I should continue, I got a glimpse of something. Something shiny in the distance got my attention. I decided that the little boy in me wanted to see what was shining in the distance so I chose to push through the pain and challenges of climbing up and down these boulders. I began to realize that I wasn't as bad off as I thought. I remembered that the adventure of climbing and pushing through wasn't always painful. I began to be filled with hope, curiosity, excitement for what was next.

When we are in the valley, sometimes letting God lead us as his child allows us to experience those things I mentioned—hope, joy, curiosity, excitement. We begin to discover a God who is bigger than we ever imagined and even in the painful moments his healing covers us in greater ways than we ever dreamed of.

I pushed all the way through and as I broke through the clearing I realized I had reached the base of one of the most amazingly beautiful and surreal places on the earth. The shining I saw was the sun shining on the base of El Capitan's granite. I was completely overwhelmed with many emotions. I had overcome some challenges that would be simple for most people but for me, they were huge. I had pushed through and I was where I wanted to be. In that place, the worship began to flow. I put my hand on the rock and began to weep as I sensed God's presence with me. I was alone so who cared? I wanted to be in this moment and so I sat there for a long time just laying against the rock that was smooth and warm from the sun. I had pushed through and now I was enjoying God's creation as a reward.

This verse is so alive for me today because of that experience:

> *"May the God of hope fill you with all joy and peace as you trust in him, so that you may overflow with hope by the power of the Holy Spirit." -Romans 15:13, NIV*

On that day, I experienced hope. I was so broken inside and had felt so alone in that place. It was something I felt almost every day while in ministry—broken and alone. You would think that I'd feel even more alone at the base of a huge mountain but I've never felt so close to my Creator, my Abba Father. I was truly filled with joy and peace. It was so intense at that moment, I've literally been sitting here trying to find the words to describe it. You had to be there.

When we choose to push through and embrace every part of each valley moment we will experience that powerful, indescribable peace that passes all human understanding. You may not be feeling much hope, happiness, peace, or grace at this time and that's ok. It's understandable. When we as leaders hurt or are spiritually dry or burned out, those feelings of rawness are real and deep. We have exposed nerves and the air is hitting them. It burns, stings, and hurts all at the same time. But, if you push through this season, you will come to a place where you are experiencing what Romans 15 is telling us.

So what are you facing in these moments? What are you needing to push through during this valley season? Is it a renewal of your ministry calling? Is it dealing with disappointments or unfulfilled expectations? Did you get blindsided or did you see this coming? Why are you finding yourself here? Don't stop asking as it might not be clear yet but it will become clearer in time.

We all will have God show us things during the valley season. We can choose to bury those things, run away from them, or push all the way through. Then we can experience the awesomeness of looking up to the top of the mountain and saying, "I'm here. I'm ready. Lead me through the valley to whatever you have

## DON'T IGNORE THE "WHY" OF THE VALLEY

for me."

My reason for pushing this so hard is clear: Before you move into something new you must deal with the wounds. You must deal with the burnout. If you don't this will get much worse and you won't last like you think. The repercussions could be even worse if you choose to give up instead of pushing through.

If you are in between ministry positions, please take time to walk through any hurt, anger, exhaustion, unhealthy boundaries, etc, before you move into the next place. I see far too many leaders who only put a Band-aid on and then ultimately reopen their wound because it hasn't had time and space to properly heal. We do a disservice to ourselves and to the ministry when we limp along with open wounds instead of allowing them to fully heal.

You may have scars but they are better than open wounds and that makes a big difference in your future. Believe me when I say this, as I have personal experience. I watched a leader who I would have run through walls for, melt down and quit ministry because he had unresolved hurts. He hadn't taken the time to work through those wounds. He mistakenly believed, as most leaders do, that they should just move to a new ministry and those old wounds would be healed and forgotten.

The problem is, he hadn't healed from those wounds and in one nasty conversation a person who had a disagreement with him, said some hurtful words and bam! the wound burst open and he "bled" and then quit.

That totally changed the path of the ministry he led and hit me personally and deeply. It also cost me my ministry too. I wasn't able to stay on staff and that was devastating.

Your "why" will be different from mine and from the "why" of others and that is fine. God created us unique and special and we are going to experience this life differently from each other. What matters is that you pursue your why and gain clarity and perspective. Learn the lessons of the valley and then look forward to living them out as you go up to the mountaintop.

# pause by the stream

If you sense you're emotionally dry, who can you talk to?

_____

_____

_____

What do you sense caused this dry spell?

_____

_____

_____

_____

What scares you about talking to someone about these deep places of the heart?

_____

_____

_____

_____

Why would the enemy not want you looking deeper?

_____

_____

_____

_____

## DON'T IGNORE THE "WHY" OF THE VALLEY

What would life look like on the other side of dryness? Describe it.

_____

_____

_____

_____

_____

_____

Are you trying to take the simple, easy path or are you ready to push through?

_____

_____

_____

_____

What are the steps you need to take to get your hands open and your heart right?

_____

_____

_____

_____

## chapter seven
# WHAT LESSONS CAN BE LEARNED IN THE VALLEY?

When your heart is ready to learn, you begin to seek God and ask the right questions. You have to want to truly understand what is going on in and around you so that you can learn all that God desires to teach. Ultimately, this process is one of refinement. God is making you into the image of himself in a greater way. He wants you to reflect on him.

So what questions do you ask?

I start with some of the same questions I mentioned earlier.

- Why am I here?
- What is he preparing me for?
- What wounds need healing?
- What boundaries need to be set-up or reinforced?
- What is next?

This new path may be to a new ministry. It may be a change in where you are or what you're doing. It may be something that you never dreamed of doing before that will stretch you. He may be leading you to a new place to serve in a new way. Ultimately you want your heart to be receptive to this new path.

I have been amazed by how many leaders say, "I'm called to ministry, but I don't want to serve in this position or that position. I'm called to the ministry, but I won't go there. I want to stay put." If that is your heart and you've said those things, let me be the first (or maybe not the first) to warn you. That is a sign you may be heading for a rockslide moment. I would challenge you. If you are called to serve God, don't put limits on where and how you will serve.

Who am I to tell God what path I should be on or what my ministry role should be?

# VALLEYS OVER MOUNTAINS

*But who are you, O man, to talk back to God? Shall what is formed say to him who formed it, 'Why did you make me like this?' Does not the potter have the right to make out of the same lump of clay some pottery for noble purposes and some for common use? -Romans 9:20, NIV*

I don't see anywhere in Scripture where the one being sent ever told the sender, "Here are my conditions for serving. If I don't get this, I'm not going."

This might be why you are experiencing a valley moment as God wants to expose this in you and allow you a gentle time to remove the conditions to your calling and instead be willing to be moved by him. Sometimes our desire to stay where we are can be a hindrance to where the Father wants to lead us.

I will also say this, and it may seem like I'm contradicting myself; There are times it's reasonable to ask God to provide something where we are. If the desire of your heart is one that is focused on others such as caring for family, etc. I can see that being something different than just personal preference or an unwillingness to move.

Paul stated in 1 Timothy 5 as he gave instructions concerning the care of widows that, "caring for their own family and so repaying their parents and grandparents, for this is pleasing to God." So if there is a reason to stay in a location for the sake of caring for family, I can fully support that.

All that aside, you have to ask yourself in this season of walking in the valley, "Am I fully in?"

Read through Romans 12:1

*Therefore, I urge you, brothers, in view of God's mercy, to offer your bodies as living sacrifices, holy and pleasing to God—this is your spiritual act of worship.*

Ask yourself, have I given it all? Am I willing to sacrifice my comfort and convenience, dreams and desires to follow where he leads me? Am I in a place where I am teachable? Am I willing to be taken out of my comfort zone?

I had to ask myself these questions when I was in the valley. I also asked myself,

## WHAT LESSONS CAN BE LEARNED IN THE VALLEY?

"Am I truly willing to do ministry even if it looks nothing like what I think it should?" Let that sit for a while before you answer.

Have I given all the hurts, disappointment, fear, and doubt over to God? The answers to questions such as these are often discovered in the valley so make sure you take the time to not only face them head on but answer them. If there are hurts in your life that you have not dealt with and you move on from the valley, odds are they will come back and, when they do, it will hurt worse and cause more damage.

You must learn the right lessons and have the answers so that you can move forward with the proper perspectives, boundaries, and priorities. Don't leave the valley without having these written down somewhere. If you're not sure what those look like, pause now and do some seeking to get clarity.

Will you always be led to a new ministry position or away from what you're currently doing? Not necessarily. In fact you may be asked to stay where God called you and continue what he called you to do. I don't want you to assume valleys are always position related, meaning that they happen in between ministry positions. Sometimes they are but other times they are not. I know people who have been in positions for 20 plus years in the same place who still ended up in valley times. Length of stay doesn't always mean it's a total breeze. Ask a leader who has served long term somewhere. They will tell you they had seasons of mountaintops and seasons in the valley. Every leader will experience both, it's not a matter of if, it's more of when.

The lessons of the valley are so many and so different that I think it would take a lifetime to write them all. I've only chosen a few that I personally have experienced or have learned about from studying so many leaders over the years.

Another lesson that came from the valley for me was to examine my ambitions. As a young pastor, my ambition was to grow the ministry, but it was also to be noticed by others. Some of my internal motivations were definitely selfish and prideful. I was envious of those in larger churches and those who got the invitation to speak. I've mentioned some of this in other chapters so I won't labor the point here too long, but if you are going to learn the right lessons, you need to study the right things.

# VALLEYS OVER MOUNTAINS

Understanding what your ambition is aimed at is a very important lesson to learn. Lance Witt shares a definition by Andrew Murray in his book, *"Replenish,"* Murray says this about having humility, *"It is the displacement of self by the enthronement of God. Where God is all, self is nothing."*

I was strongly encouraged to do a deeper study on how Jesus sees me and how God the Father sees me. When you come to a better understanding of your biblical identity in Christ it brings a sacred humility to your life. You begin to realize that your ambitions must be kept in check by the Spirit of God. When we do this, he will open doors and bless our lives and ministries in ways we cannot imagine.

If you struggle with the need for approval by others, I would encourage you to study that in Scripture as well. Begin to live for the approval of God alone and see what it does for you.

What God has for you in this valley season is for you to discover as you walk side by side with the Spirit. My best advice is to set up some days and label them, "shut up and listen day." I know that some don't like those words, but it is hard to deny we need to hear them sometimes.

We sometimes need to be quiet and listen before we can hear what God wants to share with us. We need to remember his calling in our lives and what he declares about us, not what we keep telling him we want to do or accomplish. So the lesson to be learned in the valley? Talk less, listen more.

# pause by the stream

Are you giving it everything?

_____

_____

_____

_____

Are you truly willing to sacrifice all your "wants?"

_____

_____

_____

_____

What keeps you in your comfort zone and is it worth the risk of missing God's amazing blessing?

_____

_____

_____

_____

# chapter eight
# WHAT IS IN MY LIFE?

We have made being a workaholic a badge of honor, and I don't know why. I think it's terrible.

We walk around each other and ask "how are you doing?" and we answer, "I'm exhausted." We say it like we're bragging though. We then rattle off all the things we are doing and how full and overbooked our calendars are and how little time we've taken off like a collection of trophies.

When I ask leaders about their priorities, I almost always get the "Sunday School" type answers: "God, Family, Ministry, Friends, Hobbies." Then I usually follow up by asking, "if God would speak audibly, would he agree? If I ask your family would they say this is true? Does your calendar prove your statement?" I think you're getting the point now. Often what we say doesn't really line up with how things actually are.

When we put the work we do in front of who we are it is an idol. I know that sounds legalistic but I believe it's true and I've been guilty of it. I have to admit my priorities were way out of line and I still suffer some of the consequences of this. It's one of the reasons I've pushed myself to write this little book. I don't want other leaders to fall into this trap.

Are my priorities right? The valley is a great time to ask this but don't forget to keep this question in mind when up on the mountain too. As a healthy leader, one must continually do a 360 degree evaluation and this includes a check of their priorities.

When I'm at that point, I need to say "Okay, God, how do I reshape my priorities? How do I get them back in line? Because I want to stay where you want me to be." You need to look at some of those kinds of things. Ask your family or close friends this question: "Am I doing too much? Do my priorities show up on my calendar?"

# VALLEYS OVER MOUNTAINS

Ezra gives us a simple principle, "For Ezra had devoted himself to the study and observance of the Law of the Lord, and to teaching its decrees and laws in Israel." (Ezra 7:10 NIV)

There are three principles that show up in one little verse.

His priority was to:

   1. Learn God's Word.
   2. Observe it. (This means live it.)
   3. Teach it.

Pure and simple. If you've lost your way, go back to the basics and learn it, live it, teach it. period.

Once you start getting the simplest of priorities right, the others begin to fall into place. When you devote yourself to learning God's Word it transforms everything. We have become a society of leaders who would rather Google or Amazon our answers instead of opening the original book of knowledge and faith, the Bible!

You don't have to crowdsource how to have biblical priorities? You don't have to Google, "how do I get balance in ministry?" It's in his book. check it out.

If you're someone who falls into the "people-pleaser" category oftentimes you will let others set your priorities for you because you can't say "no" to anything. Your real priority is to please people and keep them happy. That's dangerous for sure. You need solid priorities in life to navigate and help you see what you will and won't do. It does matter. If you are going to be a godly leader you must remember that leadership is always inside-out. This means that what we have going on inside will always come out of us as we lead.

Here's a bonus insight that hit me while I was working on this book: Sometimes you are brought to the valley because the Father knows you need rest.

I know, earthshaking thought right? But seriously, our God values us as his creation and he didn't design us to try to outwork him. Did you consider the fact that Jesus took naps? One example was in Mark 4:38 (NIV) "Jesus was in the stern, sleeping on a cushion. The disciples woke him and said to him, 'Teacher, don't you care if we drown?'"

Jesus was tired. He was human after all, and after spending a day around a mob of people ministering to them, he was physically tired. So when he was tired, he slept. In a boat! During a storm! I'd call that seriously tiring!

Jesus rested. He took time away from crowds. He took time away from his disciples. I think the principle is very clear that if he made it a priority to care for himself and rest, we must follow suit. We must schedule time to rest and do it. It is critical for us to be who he designed us to be and we cannot do the work of the ministry if we are always running on empty.

If your priorities get out of alignment, they can lead you to many places you don't want to be and the ministry will be hindered. Use valley times to learn to set boundaries and priorities and a system to hold and keep you accountable so that you don't get out of alignment.

Another reason for ending up in the valley, and a reason some never leave the valley, is burnout. They've lost their joy, their passion, their hope, their love for others. Their boundaries, priorities, even their calling can be lost in a season of burnout.

If you are not careful, you can let yourself wander into that valley area or you can push yourself until you fall down the mountainside and land in it with a crash! Neither are good. You don't want to find yourself here in this condition but many do. I did. I experienced it both ways as I look back and am totally honest. Parts of me I let wander into burnout and parts of me just came crashing down hard into it.

No matter how you enter burnout, it hurts. It really hurts. Burnout is a leading reason so many leaders leave ministry and provides another motivation for me to write this book. I want to help. I know I can't completely rid leaders of it but if I can help you as you read this it will be worth it.

Burnout is often described in terms of:

1. Being tired constantly

2. Consistent lack of internal motivation
3. Mental and physical fatigue
4. Lost sense of purpose and meaning

When you start feeling burned out in ministry it can weigh heavily on you and on those around you. Sometimes we don't even realize we started wandering down the slippery slope. That's why it's so dangerous for us. Burnout lurks in our blindspot.

As a leader we are often running so hard that we excuse the physical symptoms as just part of the job so we don't stop to address them. Even when times are good, we can be moving toward burnout and not even realize it. Part of the reason for this is allowing our priorities to get messed up and having boundaries that are too soft and fail to keep us accountable in our lives.

When you are feeling burned out the valley will seem like a great place to be at first, but only because we are so messed up that we think we can escape those symptoms down here. That is another lie the enemy will try to get you to believe. I write all this from personal experience and understanding what I was like in one of my valley seasons. I was toast. I was burnt toast.

My story is terrible and I'm ashamed to share it, but I know I must because I don't want other leaders to walk through all I had to. It was hard and I almost walked away from my calling and everything I loved.

I had been serving in a place where life was good. I was leading a great team and God was blessing the ministry. Growth was happening so fast I couldn't keep up. I was a younger leader and very self confident. I ran a lot on my giftings as my fuel and used my people skills to get what I needed to make things happen. I had no clear solid priorities except the "Sunday-school" answers. God, family, church. But mine were actually the other way around, church, family, God.

I had insanely soft boundaries where I said "yes" to anything and everything that came my way. I wasn't well organized. (I'm better now but still need improvement!) I was running and gunning and little did I realize how quickly I was running myself into my first encounter with ministry burnout.

I found myself feeling more tired than normal. I wanted to stay home and watch

# WHAT IS IN MY LIFE?

tv and not go do the things I should be doing to get ready for the next event. In fact I stopped planning events and doing less ministry under the excuse I wanted to focus more on discipleship. (This was not what I planned, but what I said I planned.)

My motivation for doing ministry was lacking and I became a different person. I became critical and cynical of everyone and everything. Nothing my team did was as good as I could do it but I wouldn't really lift a finger to help them make it better because it didn't benefit me. Did I mention when you're burning out you become more selfish? Yep, you do.

It finally exploded on me when several events failed miserably and I got called into my pastor's office. He wanted to know what was going on. I told him I was just tired and off my game, but I'd snap back and be ok. He approved a vacation for me and I was ready to get away. I couldn't wait to unplug.

I went away with my family and slept the first day or two. I was so exhausted, I don't remember much from those first few days. I know I wasn't really present for my family during that time. I just wanted to lay in a chair and read, but I didn't care enough even to do that. I just wanted to stop the internal hurt and feelings of being totally spent.

The way I found to recover was to stop and take inventory. I walked through looking at all the questions we've already covered and began to pray through them asking God to show me first how he saw me. I had to know what God sees when he sees me. Eventually he showed me and I know he loves me.

Then I needed to look at how I saw myself. Who did I believe I was? What was my identity rooted in? For me I realised I was basing my identity on what I did and who acknowledged that I was good at it. I should have based it on who God sees me to be. His son, created to bring him glory through the talents and abilities he blessed me with.

Then I began to look at my priorities and boundaries and I began to see where I was allowing myself to wander and fall. At this point, I asked for some help from family and friends to hold me accountable to maintaining my priorities and to call me out when I slipped.

## VALLEYS OVER MOUNTAINS

These are things I've tried to live my life with along with regularly taking breaks, resting and worshipping. And they all came out of a valley!

How can it be that simple? I believe it doesn't have to be complex to overcome burnout. You have to make the choice to not go back into it. No one can force you there. It's your choice. You can keep living unhealthily and stay unhealthy. You can choose to live intentionally by the plan God has and be healthy.

*It's your choice!*

In this valley season do you need to

- Schedule some rest time?
- Do an electronic detox?
- Stop reading everything except your Bible for a week?

The only way we truly see what's inside of us is to have a spiritual x-ray and God's Word is the perfect instrument to show us what is wrong. When God's Word shines bright into us it shows us where we need to change so we can experience the best, most abundant life Jesus described.

> *The thief comes only to steal and kill and destroy; I have come that they may have life, and have it to the full. -John 10:10, NIV*

# pause by the stream

What are your priorities? (take your time here)

_____

_____

_____

_____

Would your family agree and your calendar prove your answers?

_____

_____

_____

_____

What needs to get more attention?

_____

_____

_____

_____

How many days do you stop to rest? (do you have unused vacation or never take vacation days)

_____

_____

_____

_____

## VALLEYS OVER MOUNTAINS

What action step can you do right now to change mis-aligned priorities?

_____

_____

_____

_____

If you've struggled with burnout, what were your warning signs/symptoms?

_____

_____

_____

_____

What do you need to do to move towards health instead of burnout?

_____

_____

_____

_____

# chapter nine
# NEW VISION FROM THE VALLEY

When you ask the right questions it opens up the heart to receive new visions and dreams for yourself and the ministry you lead. When you are embracing and learning from the valley, don't be surprised when the Spirit begins to show you new things, new dreams, new directions.

I got a new vision of the way things could be and  a new vision of where God was going to lead my volunteer community and me. It takes us being in the right place and at the right time, with the right attitude for God to show us new lessons and dreams.

**I came to realize in the valley that solitude with my heavenly father is priceless and it's also a necessity if I want to continue in fruitful ministry.**

If you're anything like me, you love being around people. Being alone is not something I enjoy. I mean, I don't like solitude. I don't like feeling alone. That is total darkness for a person like me. I understand some people love solitude but for me, as you can tell, not so much.

However, I learned that I need to have times of solitude. So how did I learn this lesson? I'm glad you asked, because if you can't tell, I love telling stories.

I learned that solitude is great while walking alone in Yosemite. The first time I was challenged to do a "solitude hike" I wasn't especially happy about walking out in the wilderness in Yosemite. I'm a big guy and I'm thinking, "Yeah, you know, a bear is gonna look at me and  say to himself after a long winter hibernation, 'Hey look, a moving buffet!'" Yikes! I didn't want to become lunch for a bear so the idea of being alone was a fearful one. But down deep, I was less afraid of dealing with a bear than I was of having to deal with myself. When you are dealing with yourself, there's nobody to outrun.

I also found out that in solitude, God just speaks so softly, tenderly and clearly.

# VALLEYS OVER MOUNTAINS

I didn't hear any audible voice, but what I sensed in my spirit that day was so clear and unmistakable. His voice to my heart, "while you're down here, just be my son. Just walk with me and know that I love you and have great plans for your life." That's good! For the first time in a long time I was hearing God speak to my heart and for the first time in a long time I was listening instead of doing all the talking.

It took the valley to remind me to stop talking and start listening.

So when was the last time you made time for solitude? I am not just talking about sitting in your car, or in your house, or even in your office solitude. I'm talking about getting out alone, away from civilization and other people. For me that's what it took. I needed to fully unplug from all electronics. I needed to shut off the music. I needed to get away and out of my comfort zone. I needed that solitude like Jesus had when he went up on the mountain to spend time with his Father. You need that time as well to hide in the cave like Elijah and hear the still small voice.

If you are like me you don't like silence as much as you don't like solitude. The practice of silence in solitude is powerful for us to practice. It's something I have come to learn and believe is key to experiencing the beauty of the valley.

I will tell you that this can be painful and difficult if, like many in ministry, you have the "gift of gab" and fill silence with talk. Most people eventually get really uncomfortable with silence and being alone but some do this faster than others. But God uses times of solitude for our good.

How do we stop and listen?

For me this time of solitude and silence became a time of training. I have learned some valuable truth when it comes to silence and solitude. I would encourage you to dig into the topic for yourself. Richard Foster in his book, *Celebration of Discipline* has a great chapter on Solitude. Let me share a couple of things I gleaned from it.

First, without silence you won't experience real solitude. They go together and we need to be more intentional about fostering them as a spiritual discipline.

# NEW VISION FROM THE VALLEY

Second, Jesus was very intentional about the practice himself, there are numerous passages in scripture that point to him taking time out from daily life and ministry to go for some solitude time. It was a regular practice for him especially after being with large groups.

For us leaders, we need to take the cue that when we are running hard and ministry is filling our calendar, that we intentionally follow that season with a season of solitude, rest and refilling, just as Jesus did.

Third, what I've been calling the valley season, Foster calls the "dark night of the soul." It is the season where God draws us to a place of release. He wants you to give him your full attention and allow him to feed your soul. So that's why I've said from the beginning, embrace this valley season and you will hear God speak.

This has to happen in order for us to be ready to receive what God has for us next. If you are unwilling to endure this process, I say this in love, you are not ready for what God has next.

> *Therefore, since we are surrounded by such a great cloud of witnesses, let us throw off everything that hinders and the sin that so easily entangles, and let us run with perseverance the race marked out for us. -Hebrews 12:1, NIV*

What do you need to throw off? What is hindering you right now? Is there sin that has you entangled? I discovered that to pursue God I had to be real and open. I had to allow the Spirit to do some deep soul work in my life. I had to stop and let go of some things I had been carrying for years. I had hurt and bitterness, broken expectations, and so much more.

While in this time of solitude I knew I needed to confess what I'd been carrying far too long. I had to submit my heart to the Spirit and agree with God that I needed forgiveness for myself.

> *If we confess our sins, he is faithful and just and will forgive us our sins and purify us from all unrighteousness. -1 John 1:9, NIV*

I confessed it all to my loving Father. He allowed me to walk through all the deep emotion and all the deep pain to come and receive his love, grace and complete forgiveness for myself. I even came to a place that I never expected where I could offer forgiveness.

So when do we stop and listen?

You need to start now. It takes an intentional and hard stop of everything. I don't know of any other way. If you say, "I don't have time to stop everything and go to Yosemite!" I agree. I'm not saying you have to go out there. (But, if I could, I'd be out there a lot!) You don't have to "go to Yosemite" but you do have to be willing to stop.

I think if we are not willing to do this we have made our jobs an idol because it's become more important than our relationship with the Father. Seriously, you can stop everything and step aside for a day or two. Believe it or not, the ministry will still be there. But if you don't do this the cost can be extremely high and dangerous.

During my "solitude hike" I shut off my music and I started focusing on creation. I focused on scripture. It was incredible. Once I started, it didn't take long before the Spirit was bringing verses to my mind. It was an amazing time of worship that brought clarity.

For you, your "Yosemite" may be a fresh way of doing your time of worship or time in the Word. Sometimes in the valley you discover new ways of doing things.

Make some intentional choices to give yourself some solitude and silence and listen for that still small voice and during that time you may discover some brand new things. You may rediscover some old ones too.

Schedule time to just get alone. Get out of the noise. For me nature is my thing, for other people that would totally freak them out. Then you need to go sit in a library or a city park somewhere and be quiet. Find a coffee shop in another town and sit in the corner. Location doesn't matter as much as you being intentional and setting aside time.

I encourage people to take time to pray and fast. When I say pray, that doesn't mean talk AT God. It means just sitting and listening. I think when you pursue

# NEW VISION FROM THE VALLEY

God, it means leaning into him, worshiping him, listening to him.

We ultimately must change the image of leaders from always running and gunning to humbly walking and serving in a way that shows the Spirit's control in our life and ministry. There doesn't have to be a bunch of us walking around wounded, burned out, broken, and bitter.

So how can this happen? How can you and I break the cycle?

Start with what Lance Witt, in his book called, *Replenish* addresses. It is something he calls "image management." Image management is what we begin to do when our inner world becomes separated from our outer world."

Jesus was consistent in his pointing out how the Pharisees were all about their image management. Their fancy clothing, fancy prayer boxes. Their loud boisterous prayers when they gave their tithes. They loved the show and we do too. So many leaders are in total pursuit of the bigger and better job assignment or title. They want a role at the "big-name" church. Many of these churches are wonderful places but some are just a pretty outer image. I don't say this to say that all larger or multi-site churches are badly dysfunctional. I say it because so many ministers and churches are focused on image management because internally dysfunction, discouragement, frustration are the norm. I was in a place that was highly dysfunctional and the staff turnover was all too high and normalized there. It was not a healthy staff culture and I realized, if I stayed there, I was heading for implosion myself.

To keep my soul healthy, I must continually follow the Spirit lead. It's about him and not me anyway. To break the cycle we must lay image management aside and make sure our inner self reflects the one who designed us.

**Take some time to pause and create your Yosemite moment.**

**If you need help, check out www.restoringleaders.org This ministry is all about walking alongside leaders to help them push through the hurt and burnout struggle to journey on fully restored.**

# pause by the stream

Open your calendar: pick a day and time you will schedule some solitude and silent time.

What does it make you feel when you think about having time alone with God?

_____

_____

_____

_____

When was the last time you had any significant time to be alone and focus just on you and Jesus?

_____

_____

_____

Why is that so challenging to do?

_____

_____

_____

_____

Will you commit right now to doing so on a regular basis, spending time alone in worship, rest and restoration?

_____

_____

# chapter ten
# HE'LL CALL YOU UP!

What is it like when God calls you back to the mountaintop? What is it like when we're coming out of this place of hurt or burnout? What does it look like to be back on that mountain top? What are some things that we can look forward to?

Let's look again to Scripture in the story of Moses. You will find a couple of things that happened to him.

1. He was up on the mountain.
2. He found himself in a valley period.
3. He embraced his valley period.
4. God called him back up to meet him at a burning bush.
5. God sent him out on a new mission.

That's why I tell leaders when you're in that valley, your eyes don't always have to stay in the valley. You need to look up. You'll know when it's time. Our God doesn't want us to just wander around in the valley. As you walk with him and gain clarity of who he is and his plan for your life, you will sense when it's time to look up to the mountaintop again.

What does that look like? As you look up you will eventually begin to see a clear path back up. Wait on God. He will make it clear and give you peace.

*For God is not a God of disorder but of peace. -1 Corinthians 14:33, NIV*

When he directs you, you may not see every curve in the path to the mountaintop but you will see a clear path.

*Your word is a lamp to my feet and a light for my path. -Psalm 119:105, NIV*

You've been through the preparation, You have taken steps to prepare your heart and mind and receive what God has for you. During this time the Spirit has done his work on you. He has molded and reshaped you into someone he can fill and use for his glory.

You have taken the time to look at your boundaries and your priorities and you've lined them up with Scripture and the way God wants you to minister. You (helped by others) have remembered and reaffirmed your calling to ministry and your "why" for ministry.

You have now clearly defined the kind of leader you are designed to be and you are totally comfortable in your own skin. You're done with the comparison games. Today you know who you are. You belong to God. You are not going to be a slave to fear. You're going up and God will show you his path.

Hiking uphill is hard but I found that hiking downhill is sometimes harder. It hurts when you've been hiking and you start going downhill but, at times, going uphill can be so refreshing.

When will he call you back up? When his timing is perfect for you, that's when. Don't get focused on a timeline or a process, including this one. The journey is the goal, not the destination. We get so focused on where we need to go and how long it takes but this process is not about how much time it takes to journey through. It's about learning and growing and if that takes an extended length of time then let it be.

Don't you believe the Father has the best of intentions for you? Do you believe he wants you to experience the full life? He does, of course, but that doesn't mean it will happen on your timetable or your plan.

Don't rush this process and don't just rush the valley experience. I'll let you in on a secret. You can't, even if you try. I've said this several times, "trust me, I know." That is because I do.

There have been several seasons I've tried to rush through the valley, but every time you are there you just have to focus on being in the valley and nothing more for as long as it takes. Growing impatient will only make it feel longer.

I remember hiking on a trail and wondering many times, "How much farther?" Every time I saw a sign with distances on it, they always seemed to say it was getting closer to the destination but it sure didn't feel like it. I started believing that someone was just placing signs at random points but the distances were completely inaccurate. I thought someone was messing with me.

I was too focused on the destination instead of the journey. I was focused on how long it would take and just wanted to get there. Wow, I'm thankful that during the hike a good brother and friend, Peter, reminded me that I needed to focus on my journey and what I was experiencing. I needed to embrace this journey and let it end when it ends. You can't rush a hike when you're going up and down mountains anyway. So just take one step, and another step, and keep moving forward in the right direction and enjoying the beauty.

You need to trust the Father and that he truly has the plan to order your steps and to guide you along the way. Allow this time to pass in the way it's designed to. When you start getting the life he designed for you in order, you will be in a place to hear him calling you back up. God is not a good of confusion or chaos. Psalms 37:23 and Proverbs 20:24 remind us of the following truths:

> If the Lord delights in a man's way, he makes his steps firm;
> A man's steps are directed by the Lord.
> How then can anyone understand his own way?

When we lay out our lives before God in full submission his timing is always perfect. We will not always understand his timing or his ways but we can trust them fully. When you're in the valley you see what Proverbs 3:5-6 truly mean.

> Trust in the Lord with all your heart
> and lean not on your own understanding;
> in all your ways acknowledge him,
> and he will make your paths straight

So there's our final process in this journey, I want to focus on a few of the powerful words from the vese we just read together.

## trust

Trusting in God with all our hearts means committing to what he says in his word. Don't play games with it or try to make it fit how you think it should fit.

We, as modern day believers, play too many games with God's Word. We try to contextualize and modernize it. I strongly suggest that this gets us into trouble because we want to tell God what we think his Word should mean and how we should live instead of taking it for the truth as it's written. It's fine if you disagree with me. This is my opinion. I have chosen to live my life by this path. It works for me.

# lean

Leaning not on our understanding is connected to humility. We often believe ourselves to be smarter than we are, wiser than we are, and more understanding than we are. I know I'm a fool in so many ways and one thing I've come to embrace over the years is the more I think I know and understand, the less I really truly do. I want more than anything to come to understand and gain wisdom and true knowledge that comes from the Father. I want to gain his wisdom and knowledge for my life and that comes from pursuing him with all that I have.

# acknowledge Him

When you are going through a valley season, acknowledging God is powerful. To acknowledge means "to know." Think about all your "ways," meaning everything you do, all your hopes and dreams, and desires. In all of these ways we are to know him more intimately than anything. We spend a lot of time learning things, studying new ideas but how deeply do we study God to know him? Of course, I comprehend we cannot fully "know" him. But, I argue that we can know so much more about him! He has revealed himself in his word and in his creation and we know him by knowing others and the power that's revealed in their lives because of him. We can know God deeper than we do. In these valley seasons that should be our number one focus. I just want to know you, God.

The deeper our acknowledgement of who he is, the greater our understanding of his path for us to follow and of the calling he's placed on our lives. I've just started understanding this in a deeper way as I look at those I read about in the Bible and their relationship with God. Look at Elijah and Moses, who we have learned so much from already, and we see such an intimacy with God. I wonder, can I have a relationship as deeply intimate as that? Maybe this is why I'm here in the valley. Maybe that is why you are here.

# He will make your straight path

What a comfort this is when I read this. He doesn't want us to struggle on our own to find the path. This doesn't mean it will be easy or all flat either. He says he will make it straight. I believe that to be a clear and direct path. We don't have to force our way to find it. He leads us to it and we walk in full obedience. My struggle has always been that I want to find and blaze my own path. My path would be nice and level and beautiful. But God promises a "straight" path. This straight path is one that is always leading to the right places. The path we follow is critical to fulfilling our calling and accomplishing our life's mission while on this earth. Finding the straight path requires full obedience on our part and a submission to God's plan for us.

When we are in valley seasons, as I've said before, sometimes it's for rest, renewal, and refocus. It may also be for reassignment. Reassignment can mean a call to something new. It can also mean restarting where you are, but this time doing it fully the way he wants. Don't mistake valley seasons as always having to do with getting a new job.

Sometimes ministry leaders feel most like they are in the valley when they have just left or lost their ministry position. I've had that happen, but I also have found myself in the valley because the ministry I was currently doing lost the focus that it should have had. I wandered off the straight path and found myself lost.

My prayer is that, during your valley, you find your way to the straight path God has for you. I pray you discover this time is for your good and can help you keep what is the most important at the top, now and forever.

# pause by the stream

What is God speaking to you about now?

_____

_____

_____

_____

_____

_____

What changes do you need to make?

_____

_____

_____

_____

_____

_____

What steps do you need to take to reset priorities? Boundaries?

_____

_____

_____

_____

_____

_____

# HE'LL CALL YOU UP!

What clarity do you have regarding a new ministry vision?

_____

_____

_____

_____

Is there anything God showed you that you need to stop doing?

_____

_____

_____

_____

Who do you need to set up some accountability with?

_____

_____

Write down the dream/plan/action steps on your path. (You may not know every step but write down what you do see clearly that you need to do.)

_____

_____

_____

_____

_____

_____

# chapter eleven
# WHAT DOES A MOUNTAIN TOP LOOK LIKE?

The mountains, as I describe them, are places where you're functioning in your strengths and seeing wins all over the place. You're in the zone! You're hearing God speak and you're following what he's doing. It's stuff that you can't explain, which is always the best place to be. Do you remember your first day of ministry? Remember the joy, excitement, the overwhelming number of dreams and desires running 24/7 through your heart and mind? Yep, that's what being up on the mountaintop is like. Day One!

When you're up on the mountain, you are leading others to do more and reach more. God is at work all around. (But remember, we have learned he's doing the same kinds of work in the valley)

The mountaintop times are where you feel you're doing exactly what God has designed you to do. You are leading others to discover God and his plan for their lives as well. It is a wonderful place to live and serve, but it's not the only place to be. I have learned that there are beautiful lessons to be learned in both places. Both places can draw you closer to the God who loves you and designed you. He provides protection for you as you journey. Consider Psalm 139:5-8

> You hem me in—behind and before; you have laid your hand upon me.
> Such knowledge is too wonderful for me, too lofty for me to attain.
> Where can I go from your Spirit? Where can I flee from your presence?
> If I go up to the heavens, you are there; if I make my bed in the depths, you are there.

The word "hem" means to siege or besiege. God literally lays siege to our lives in such a way that he provides what we need when we need it. When we need his overwhelming presence in the valley, he is there. When we need him up on the mountaintops, he is there!

# VALLEYS OVER MOUNTAINS

**I truly believe that valleys can be better than mountaintops.**

Mountaintops are beautiful places to serve. You grow yourself as a leader and you can really develop and see others do the same. Mountaintops are places of great growth, but they are just different from the valleys. People often think that going into the valley is a negative thing. I want to show that this is wrong thinking.

I hired my first ministry coach when I was on a mountaintop. Things were going well, but I knew I had to grow more to help our ministry grow more. I understood John Maxwell's principle, the "law of the lid." If you don't know what this is, I highly recommend you read Maxwell's book, "The Twenty-One Irrefutable Laws of Leadership" Very simply it states, *"Your leadership ability will always determine your effectiveness."*

Even on an amazing mountaintop you need to keep growing and developing your skills as a leader.

When you are on the mountaintop, soak it all in. Dig deeper into how close you feel to the Father. See all that his hand has created for you and gain a higher perspective for what you give your life towards. Stay humble and gracious and remember who is the great source of your blessings. It is not your effort or talent or ability that brings beauty. It is purely the Father working in and through you.

When we are forgetful of these truths we can fall from the mountain. We can take things for granted or become discontented that we aren't at a high enough elevation. We do things so people will notice us and what we are doing. I've seen leaders who built their "kingdom" on the mountain. Please don't go that route. You'll fall too.

For the longest time I wanted to be noticed. I wanted the invitations to speak at the big conferences. I had people telling me I should be doing those things. I WANTED more. I began to believe I deserved more.

I've shared this earlier in this book. My personal desire to be known became a distraction to receiving the mountaintop blessings. I started to compare my mountain to other leaders' mountains (that is never good). Whenever you find yourself comparing yourself to others, you need to hit a hard stop. You need to spend some time with the Father and let him show you your value and your path.

If you find yourself in this place, it's a good time to pause by the stream. Do some reflection and get to the root of why you want to be known like that? Do you really believe that it's worth risking what God has for you instead of resting in the fact you are known by him?

Living on the mountaintops is a blessing and shouldn't be taken for granted. We aim to serve God no matter whether we are in a valley or up high. Sometimes we think that the best ministry happens up on the mountaintops but I have experienced some amazing things even in the valley. That's why I often say that valleys are better than mountaintops. No matter where you are and what season you're in, by keeping your heart in the right place and focusing on the right things, you will experience the fullness of his Spirit and the power of who he is.

There is no doubt that being up on a mountain looking down on the beauty of the valley is incredible and breathtaking. It is the same kind of feeling as when you see someone step across the line of faith or take their next step on their journey with Christ. When you feel this way, you know you're in the right place at the right time. s. When you don't feel this way, pause by a stream and check your heart and soul. You need to see things from God's perspective when you're on the mountain too. You shouldn't allow the location of your ministry to be something that gives you security as you are replaceable. I encourage you to stay humble and teachable. Let God bring security to your life by living in your calling.

Take a heart check daily. Let the Spirit lead you through it. As you dig deeper into your Bible, allow the Spirit to teach you and show you how to minister the way Jesus would have you to minister. Don't do something just because someone else thinks it's a good idea.

Don't just jump from strategy to strategy or program to program. That is dangerous for you and for those you lead. God is a God of order and steps, so take steps after seeking him and let the peaks and smaller valleys be refreshing and renewing.

## VALLEYS OVER MOUNTAINS

One thing I have discovered while walking the path on the mountaintop is that you learn to look forward and around more. What I mean by that is, as you learn to lead yourself well, you become more aware that looking forward is important not only to your ministry but to yourself. If you spend most of your time looking in other directions you will probably trip and fall. When we walk, we are to walk wisely with our eyes forward. There will be times to stop, reflect, look around, and look back to where we came from, but the first priority is to keep our eyes forward.

Why is this so important? Because it keeps you from walking backwards or going off the path, and it keeps you moving in the right direction with the right focus and the right pace. When you see what's ahead, you know if you need to increase your speed, slow down, or even stop and rest a while. There are leaders just starting out in ministry who think they can run up every mountain. Sure for a short time you can, but after a while you learn that pacing means everything when climbing up mountains. The right pace means you can sustain something good.

I learned hard lessons about pacing in ministry and how it helps keep me up where I belong. When I was much younger and had lots of dreams and ideas, I was always thinking so much about what was next that I often didn't finish what I had started. I was running onto the next thing I wanted to achieve. It didn't matter to me that I was outrunning my team, my leaders, my family, or even myself. I wanted to reach the next peak.

Many leaders fall into the unhealthy belief that ministry life is about how many peaks you climb. They want to build a resume. Is that really the ultimate goal of life and ministry? I certainly believe that is a big fat NO! I believe that what God wants for us to be and to do is to be the best followers of Jesus we can possibly be. He desires us to become so much like him that we think and live just like him. We should minister at a pace that he would take. We model that pace for others and we should sustain it in a healthy way.

When we try running up every peak, we will grow tired. I know I shared this earlier about switchbacks in the mountains. But I learned another lesson there that is applicable to this section. I remember as I was hiking this very steep grade that there were what felt like endless switchbacks. It was getting hot, it was dusty. We were at a much higher elevation than I'd ever been and it was getting to me. As I came to each corner of the switchback I would pause to bring my heartrate down to a safe level and sip a bit of water and give myself another pep talk about why I was doing this. Why? Because I wanted to see what was next. I wanted to experience more of the beauty up close than I had seen from the other side of the valley. The only way to reach that destination was to stay on the path, maintain a healthy pace, and keep going.

As we were walking and stopping on the corners and especially if there was some shade, I noticed there were others coming up the path. I decided to let them pass as I could tell they were moving faster anyway. Then I was shocked. There were about four monks hiking together. They were barefoot! Well they wore these thin leather sandals, and might as well have been barefoot!

They were coming up the switchbacks at a quick pace and I couldn't believe it. They had their round hats, a small container of water and that was it. No backpack, no 32 ounce camelbak water supply, or noticeable trail snacks. They were just trucking up that mountain like it was nothing and smiling at us with our hiking boots, big backpacks, 64 ounces of water, and my wonderful trail snacks!

I stood there dumbfounded as I watched them disappear. How could they manage such a feat? How could they sustain that kind of pace up this mountain? And an even bigger question, would they join together and just carry me up the mountain??

I spent some time reflecting on this and came back with these thoughts.

**First principle:** walk at a sustainable pace. They knew what their healthy pace was and they walked it. They did it with such joy in their eyes and on their faces. So first thought for us: Do we minister that way? Do we lead ourselves that way? Do we walk the path for us on the mountain in a sustainable way?

**Second principle:** carry only what you need. Are you carrying more than you need? I realized that for a day hike, even if it was to be all day, I didn't really need all the supplies I was carrying. I had stuff for every contingency that I could imagine but the odds of ever needing them were as likely  as getting those monks to carry me up the mountain.  Often in ministry we strap ourselves to too many tasks and believe we can truly carry it all and sustain a running pace up the mountain. We cut through switchbacks and think that too is wise. I will most certainly tell you cutting through is more exhausting than following the longer path of the switchback. (that's basically straight up hill, people!) I now live my life carrying less.

I am always tempted to pick up more and add it to my load but I know what my sustainable pace is and what is necessary to live out my life's mission. I don't have to join every club, facebook group, conference, etc. I don't need every app for my phone or the newest and brightest technology to be effective in ministry. I need a sustainable pace and a lighter load.

**Third principle:** When you stop, seek God to clarify what you are really gifted to do and how to focus those gifts. He shows you the mountaintop path to follow where pace and load matter but they also help you keep going.

God uses seasons like this to show you life, balance, growth, new visions, new ways of ministry that may not even be traditional methods. He speaks in soft whispers and because you are walking and not running you can hear him speak.

Will there be seasons that one or all of these can change or become greater? Absolutely there will be. There will be times to run hard. There will be times you need to look back or around you. There will be times for you to carry more because others can't themselves. But I have seen in those seasons that God provides the switchbacks or he lets us come to a stream or a place of shade and rest where we can sit and catch up and renew our strength without self destructing or hurting others.

Talk to some more experienced leaders and ask them about these three principles in their lives? I think most would agree that these are vital to longevity in ministry. All of these have long reaching effects into our spiritual, emotional and physical lives.

I want to encourage you in your journey to spend some significant time considering what health looks like with these three areas for you. Seek God on this. Get wise counsel from others. Proverbs 15:22 says, "Plans fail for a lack of counsel, but with many advisors they succeed."

# pause by the stream

What are some things you need to praise God for?

_____

_____

_____

_____

What has God increased in your own leadership/ministry?

_____

_____

_____

_____

What priorities have you kept strong and what has slipped down the list in importance?

_____

_____

_____

_____

Have you been guilty of comparing your ministry to others?

_____

_____

_____

# VALLEYS OVER MOUNTAINS

Where has your focus been lately? Forward, backward, sideways, down? Why?

_____

_____

_____

_____

Do you feel your pace of life has been a healthy one? Why or why not?

_____

_____

_____

_____

Is the ministry load you carry sustainable at a healthy pace? What do you need to give up to make it healthy if it's not?

_____

_____

_____

_____

What scripture comes to mind as you reflect on these ideas and why do you think the Spirit is causing you to think about them?

_____

_____

_____

_____

_____

# chapter twelve
# HOW DO I KEEP THE LESSONS LEARNED IN THE VALLEY WHILE ON THE MOUNTAINTOPS?

I often get asked by leaders, "how do you keep the lessons you learned in the valley?" For me there are several things I must do to make sure I don't lose the valley experience. I must make the lessons part of my life and use them as guides to stay on the right path. Let me share a few of them with you.

When you look back into your valley experiences you see clearly some of the things that got you there.

One way to keep the lessons I have learned that sometimes you just gotta say no. You do this by keeping a "to-don't" list. A "to-don't" list is things you will not do and you delegate to others that have the gifts to do these things better.

I also had to learn how to say "no" even to my senior leader. (You can't do this unless you establish boundaries, priorities, and accountability.)

Another way to keep valley lessons is control of your calendar. You may need to give someone "veto" power over your calendar. If you start putting too much down they can veto some things. That means you'll either be saying "no" more or delegating more. Burnout is an ugly thing and an easy place to slip back into by not controlling your pace and calendar.

A practice that helped me was to schedule times throughout the year to "Pause by the Stream," and evaluate where I am spiritually, where I am as a husband and father, and where I am as a ministry leader. I take inventory of my boundaries and priorities to make sure they are still strong and clear. I lay out my plans for the coming days and ask God for continued confirmation that I am on the right track. I set time aside for solitude and silence. This is the best way I know to keep the lessons from the valley fresh and clear.

# VALLEYS OVER MOUNTAINS

If you desire to stay in ministry for a long time, you need to learn as soon as you can these principles,

- Keep your eyes forward.
- Maintain a sustainable pace.
- Carry the right load.
- Take someone with you.
- Keep a to-don't list.
- Take naps.
- Serve the audience of one.

This is a topic that I'm very passionate about because I'm just done with the enemy scoring wins by taking leaders out.

I want to hear more stories about people like me that have been in ministry for more than thirty years, that have learned the ministry lessons and are sharing them with others. I have learned that even when you know the lessons you are still vulnerable to rockslide moments, where you have to re-learn a lesson or two. When and if those times come I hope you can walk yourself through those seasons and come out the other side a better person for it.

By God's grace, every season has drawn me closer to my God and my family. The valley season has helped me become a better leader. The valley season is why I've dedicated my life to always giving what I know to those coming behind me. I want them to see God doing greater things. I want their ministry to be filled with trophies of grace and redemption. I want them to experience the God of the mountain and the God of the valley. The Great I AM is more and more amazing the closer you get to him and the more you experience his presence.

God will not waste your pain or experiences. He never wastes anything and they will always be for your good or for the good of those watching you as you walk through them.

I am here to tell you God is in the valley and He is on the mountaintops and He wants to meet you, lead you, walk alongside you in both places. May you enjoy the tops but learn to love the valley.

*Many nations will come and say,*

# HOW DO I KEEP THE LESSONS LEARNED...

*"Come, let us go up to the mountain of the Lord,*
*to the house of the God of Jacob. He will teach us his ways." -Micah 4:2, NIV*

# pause by the stream

Open your calendar, look out 3 months from now. Pick a day (at least a few hours) and set aside this time to "pause by the stream" for yourself.

_____

_____

If you haven't yet, get an accountability partner and show them your priorities list, boundaries list, ministry plan, and strategy. Give them your calendar and let them give you honest feedback about how these things line up and where you are not in line.

_____

_____

_____

_____

Spend some time worshiping.  Make sure to focus on just listening for God to speak: Write down any impressions you have after this time.

_____

_____

_____

_____

_____

_____

Read and meditate on these scriptures:

_I have set the Lord always before me. Because he is at my right hand, I will not be shaken. Therefore my heart is glad and my tongue rejoices; my body also will rest_

# HOW DO I KEEP THE LESSONS LEARNED...

*secure, because you will not abandon me to the grave, nor will you let your Holy One see decay. You have made known to me the path of life; you will fill me with joy in your presence, with eternal pleasures at your right hand.*
*-Psalm 16:8-11, NIV*

_____

_____

_____

_____

*Listen, my son, accept what I say, and the years of your life will be many. I guide you in the way of wisdom and lead you along straight paths. When you walk, your steps will not be hampered; when you run, you will not stumble.  Hold on to instruction, do not let it go; guard it well, for it is your life.*
*-Proverbs 4:10-13, NIV*

_____

_____

_____

_____

# bonus chapter
# TREASURE HUNTING
# WHILE IN THE VALLEY

This process of writing this book has been extremely hard for me. I'm not a natural writer. I'm a talker. It's so much easier for me to talk to people than to write my thoughts down. Writing is totally out of my comfort zone, but I truly felt like God wanted me to write to encourage leaders during the seasons that many will find very difficult.

This morning I found myself digging into Proverbs chapter two and finding some great treasure that felt totally appropriate for this moment. When you are in the valley you are on a treasure hunt. (Or at least I think you should be!) You are seeking out God and his amazing love for you and seeking to see how he sees you. Then, as you begin to develop a healthy view (God's view) of yourself, you can seek greater wisdom and understanding from this experience.

Solomon challenged his son to "turn his ear to wisdom and apply his heart to understanding." Learning to listen to wisdom and applying it so that you have understanding is critical to moving forward in this journey through the valley. Many times we want to rush this process and, as I've said before and you've read before, don't rush this experience, embrace it. Listen. Apply.

Why do I say this? Hear what Solomon would say to you if he were walking alongside you. I love how the Message Bible translates Proverbs 2:3-5

> That's right—if you make Insight your priority,
> and won't take no for an answer,
> Searching for it like a prospector panning for gold,
> like an adventurer on a treasure hunt,
> Believe me, before you know it Fear-of-God will be yours;
> you'll have come upon the Knowledge of God.

When you are walking in the valley season you have to be like an old-time prospector. Finding gold wasn't an easy process. Unlike movies, that make it look simple, it takes someone with experience (Wisdom) and someone who is willing to apply that wisdom. You have to seek it, search for it, dig for it. Gold, or wisdom, won't be sitting on the surface. When we find ourselves in these valley seasons, as we walk, we search. And sometimes we have to stop and dig.

I find myself setting times aside now in my life to intentionally dig and search for the treasure that is deep in God's Word. It is hard and it hurts and it seems confusing and yes, you will find times where you just want to quit and do something else.

Please don't.

You have to trust the Father and, while you don't know me, I'm a brother in Christ and I encourage you to lean into the wisdom I've gained from this process and journey. I may not know your circumstances that led you into this valley but I understand where you are. I know that, no matter the reason, you are here to grow and to gain deeper wisdom and understanding.

Look again at the words in Proverbs 2:4-5,

> *and if you look for it as for silver*
> *and search for it as for hidden treasure,*
> *then you will understand the fear of the Lord*
> *and find the knowledge of God.*

It says, *"if "*you look for it. You have a choice during these valley seasons to be frustrated and angry at the circumstances or to praise the God of the mountains *and* the valleys for allowing you to search for the treasure of understanding and knowledge.

The treasure that we seek is the understanding of the fear of the Lord and the knowledge of God.

What is the fear of the Lord? It is becoming someone who has a deep respect for him and who he really is. It is acknowledging him, and all that he is, in a way that you listen and apply and obey his wisdom regardless of what culture says or what is the norm of the day.

# TREASURE HUNTING WHILE IN THE VALLEY

How much do you really respect God? How diligent are you to apply his words to your daily life? What can you point to in your life that God has recently transformed to be more like him?

As I'm digging for treasure while writing this, I realize that I need to dig and search harder myself. I haven't been as diligent lately as I should be! (I am being real because this is a real battle you will face.) I need to remind myself why it's so important. This answer is revealed at the end of verse five. "Then you will understand the fear of the Lord and find the knowledge of God."

If you want understanding and knowledge, open up your heart as you walk in the valley and turn your eyes to where he wants you to look. As we do that we can expect him to honor his promise and show us some amazing things.

> For the Lord gives wisdom,
> and from his mouth come knowledge and understanding.
> He holds victory in store for the upright,
> he is a shield to those whose walk is blameless,
> for he guards the course of the just
> and protects the way of his faithful ones. -Proverbs 2:6-8, NIV

God is the one that will give you his wisdom. Knowledge and understanding come from him! The victory (beauty) of the valley he holds in store for those who are upright.

He protects you when others cause a rockslide. He is our shield. He guards your course (your path) and he protects you along the way.

This really hit me in an amazing way as I was writing this. Then a friend sent me a song entitled "Midnight" by Rita Springer. You may want to pause reading for a moment and go look up her song online.

You may be feeling that God will never show up in the valley for you. You may be sitting here in deep fear, anxiety, or depression and thinking , "sure Tom, that worked for you. You saw God in your valley, but he hasn't shown up for me yet and I've been searching and digging."

I understand that and I asked those same questions and yelled those questions many times while in a valley. "Where are you?" "When are you showing up?" Take a look at the lyrics:

*VERSE*
*You are never late*
*Even when the sun is hiding*
*You never hesitate*
*You have perfect timing*
*Even in the wait*
*You hold on tightly*
*It's reason enough for me*
*It's reason enough for me*

*CHORUS*
*Out of the shadows*
*Into tomorrow*
*You don't wait for sunrise*
*You will move at midnight (Yes You will)*
*Out of my worry*
*Nothing but worship*
*I won't wait for sunrise*
*I will praise at midnight*

*-Midnight by Rita Springer*

We often think God has to show up on our time table or in our sequence of events but that is not how our God works, is it? He shows up in his perfect time and in his perfect way. We are to seek him diligently, live in obedience daily, and walk the path he has for us so that we can see him whenever he shows up and however he shows up. It may feel like midnight to you.

There was a hike we did one year in Yosemite where we started in the dark. It was before sunrise and we were sitting in the dark on the mountaintop. It was cold at 7,000 feet in elevation. I wasn't exactly prepared for it. I was prepared to hike in the sun and warmth, not in the dark and cold. But I can tell you the beauty in the darkness is something I truly cannot fully describe. But it was as dark as midnight up there. I found my flashlight that I could put on my head so I could open up God's Word and begin my day seeking him. I was there on this retreat after all to find out why I was mentally and spiritually in a valley season.

This is where I now understand the beauty of what Rita was singing about. "I won't wait for sunrise, I will praise at midnight." In Hebrew culture, the day actually starts at the beginning of sundown. God literally begins days at sundown. He doesn't wait for the sunrise to work; he starts at the beginning of our days.. Let that soak in for a while. In our culture, the new day begins at midnight, not at sunrise!

It can feel scary sometimes to be in a valley where it feels like midnight. But God works in our valleys, during what feels like midnight when we cannot see the path. When you can only see dimly, at best, you need some light to see what's out ahead and God is the only light source you have in a valley. I again go back to The Message for the next few verses as I love how it describes what comes our way when we commit to the valley and we commit to seeking and searching. Read chapter 2:9-11

> *So now you can pick out what's true and fair,*
> *find all the good trails! Lady Wisdom will be your close friend,*
> *and Brother Knowledge your pleasant companion. Good Sense will scout*
> *ahead for danger,*
> *Insight will keep an eye out for you.*

As you prepare for the next season God has for you, let's pause.

I encourage you to dig deeper for yourself into Proverbs 2. Read it in a different translation than you normally read. I pray you see what God promises is ahead of you if you pursue what he has for you.

# pause by the stream

When it comes to seeking wisdom and understanding, why do we struggle? What keeps us from digging deeper?

_____

_____

_____

_____

_____

_____

Read Proverbs 2:1-15 and reflect. What stands out to you?

_____

_____

_____

_____

_____

_____

What Wisdom have you been given that you are struggling to act on?

_____

_____

_____

_____

_____

_____

## TREASURE HUNTING WHILE IN THE VALLEY

What are you waiting on God to show you? What unanswered questions do you have? Write them down and then seek God.

_____

_____

_____

_____

_____

_____

I pray that this book will both bless and encourage you. I pray that you will experience the power and grandeur of the mountaintops and the beauty and stillness of the valleys and that in all of that, you will come to know in a fresh way the overwhelming, never ending love of the Father.

# citations

**The First Valley Experience**

Eyre, Stephen D. Drawing Close to God: the Essentials of a Dynamic Quiet Time. InterVarsity Press, 1995.

**Don't Ignore The "Why" of Valley Moments.**

Cymbala, Jim, and Dean Merrill. Fresh Wind, Fresh Fire: What Happens When God's Spirit Invades the Heart of His People. Zondervan, 2018.

**What Lessons Can be Learned in the Valley?**

Witt, Lance. Replenish: Leading from a Healthy Soul. Baker Books, 2011.

**New Visions From The Valley**

Foster, Richard J. Celebration of Discipline: the Path to Spiritual Growth. HarperOne, 2018.

Witt, Lance. Replenish: Leading from a Healthy Soul. Baker Books, 2011.

**What Does a Mountaintop Look Like?**

Maxwell, John C. The 21 Irrefutable Laws of Leadership. Thomas Nelson, 2008.

RESTORING
LEADERS.ORG

EST.2019

Restoring Leaders is a by faith ministry that serves leaders at any level.

We aim to help leaders Refocus, Renew, and Restore so that they can lead the way they were created to lead. We do this by providing 1on1 guiding, online connection groups and in-person retreats.

If you or someone you need is struggling with burnout, being overwhelmed or you've been hurt or wounded in leadership,we are here for you.

You can learn more about all we do at:
www.restoringleaders.org

Tom Bump is available for training, speaking and consulting church teams and business leaders on the principles of leadership restoration.
www.tombump.com